TRUJILLO

BY

ABELARDO R. NANITA

SENATOR OF THE REPUBLIC,
FORMER SECRETARY OF THE
PRESIDENT, FORMER MEMBER
OF THE CABINET, ETC.

FIFTH EDITION

(REVISED AND ENLARGED)

NEW
ENGLISH VERSION

EDITORA DEL CARIBE, C. POR A.
CIUDAD TRUJILLO
1954

To

Doña Julia Molina de Trujillo

"To the sweet and self-effacing goodness of the mother, calm possessor of all virtues".

A. R. N.

OTHER PUBLISHED WORKS OF THE AUTHOR:

LA CRISIS ("THE CRISIS") (OUT OF PRINT)

UNA PROVINCIA QUE PERECE ("THE DYING PROVINCE") (OUT OF PRINT)

TRIPTICO ("TRIPTYCH") (OUT OF PRINT)

TRUJILLO DE CUERPO ENTERO ("A FULL LENGTH PORTRAIT OF TRUJILLO) (1st. 2nd, and 3rd. EDITIONS, OUT OF PRINT)

"TRUJILLO, A FULL SIZE PORTRAIT" (TRANSLATED BY M. A. MOORE)

TRUJILLO Y LA POSTGUERRA ("TRUJILLO AND THE POST - WAR WORLD") (OUT OF PRINT).

TRUJILLO (4TH. EDITION)

TRUJILLO (2nd. EDITION, IN ENGLISH)

UN HEROE DE SAN CRISTOBAL ("A Hero of San Cristobal") (BIOGRAPHICAL DATA GATHERED BY GENERAL EUSEBIO PEREYRA).

TRUJILLO (5th EDITION).

TABLE OF CONTENTS

PART THREE

THE STATESMAN

PART FOUR

TRUJILLO'S ADMINISTRATION

PART FIVE

COMMENTS

FOREWORD

I began publishing these essays in December 1932, that is sixteen months after Generalissimo Trujillo had taken the oath of office as President of the Republic for the first time. At that time I published the Silueta del Presidente Trujillo (*"A Sketch of President Trujillo"*), *my first biographical work about him, the main points of which are still valid. Since then I have devoted my entire literary output to a detailed study of the man and his work. Thus, other outlines were published as newspaper articles under various titles in the* Listin Dairio *and* La Opinion *from 1932 to 1936. In August 1937 my work* Trujillo de Cuerpo Entero (*"A Full-Length Portrait of Trujillo"*) was published, embodying new aspects *of that multi-faceted personality and completing the preceding works. The present work is a revised edition of those others that constituted the fourth edition of "Trujillo", which now appears considerably increased by other articles, some of which have been published before. I have thought it likewise appropriate to include several illustrations. At the outset of this book, by way of introduction, it has seemed fitting to give again in this edtion the biographical data that were published in 1933 in so concise a manner by the cultur-*

ed and brilliant pen of Rafael Vidal. The outstanding characteristics of Trujillo's personality are accurately set forth therein.

I have likewise prepared for this edition a brief account of our country's principal aspects from the standpoints of geography, history and politics. While Dominicans may feel that it was hardly necessary, I believe it an essential aid for non-Dominican readers if if they are to understand properly the magnitude of Trujillo's achievements.

Moreover, that account, contained in the first two chapters, provides a dramatic background for the unexpected contrasts that the reader will encounter later in the book. A mountain appears higher for the valley that surrounds it; lightning flashes most vividly in the darkness of night. Likewise Trujillo's personality is all the greater when viewed against the darkness of the past.

As the reader may appreciate, what may have seemed in 1932 to many a mere and possibly far-fetched mirage conjured by me and set in the future, is now a positive, tangible, incontestable reality. Time has proved that it was not a mirage.

Glancing backward over the years for a fuller perspective, President Trujillo's figure becomes all the more enhanced. His imposing greatness which broke through the dark clouds of our past is not of relative grandeur; it is not a bluff that seems high because of a comparison with the surrounding terrain but, rather, a lofty peak that rises high above, dominating far beyond our immediate horizons.

The upright and heroic figure of Generalissimo Trujillo has been viewed from beyond our frontiers and even our continent, and is now discussed, praised, attacked or defended by a greater number of writers of world renown than that of any other statesman or historical personage of Latin America and possibly of the world.

All the above despite the fact that, as the American writer, J. W. Vandercook, has stated in caustic criticism, the scene of his portentous activity has been merely a small Caribbean island. This remark unwittingly betrays a latent, albeit reluctant, admiration. Indeed, the geographical area of the scene of his actions is a mere pedestal for his person. The opportunity that a larger country with far greater resources might have afforded for the creative spirit, the indomitable will and the unflagging passion for progress in Trujillo defies imagination.

Much has been and is being written even now about Trujillo, the creator of peace and progress in his country; the bibliography on him is therefore extensive. Still, one cannot determine accurately which has been the culminating moment in his life.

Which has been his greatest contribution to his country's glory? Is it the Trujillo-Hull Treaty that gave it its financial independence? Is it the demarcation of the frontiers with Haiti that ended once for all the boundary disputes with that country and permitted the Dominicanization of wide areas that were ours by law if not in fact? Is it his plan for a League of American Nations, reviving Bolívar's prophetic dream? Is it the total payment of the foreign debt? Or is it the creation, the maintenance and the defense of this blessed peace which serves as a basis for all the progress achieved?

History confers upon the hero of a battle some special title. The glory of a stand taken or the eternal sublimeness of a moment are immortaliezd for posterity through art in marble, bronze or granite. But our problem is how to present in precise terms so rich, varied and intensive a life as that of Trujillo while it is still in flower.

The only loyal thing that can be done without distorting historical truth is to trace the unfolding of his personality and to examine its development, trying the while to interpret his provident plans, in order to confirm or correct impressions or opinions that, a posteriori, lend themselves to such confirmation or correction. In other words, the thing to do is to bring up to date those impressions or opinions in the clarifying light of more recent historical events. That is what I have tried to do in the present edition; I feel that it is the final and concrete expression of my definitive opinion regarding Trujillo.

I must say, however, that notwithstanding the fact that more than eighteen years have elapsed since my first article, I have not yet had to erase a single line that I wrote nor to modify or correct a single one of the opinions I expressed.

Subsequent events have borne out my conclusions.

It need not surprise anyone that in writing of Trujillo my enthusiasm should readily cause me to praise him. I am a sincere admirer of his accomplishments which I am able to evaluate, in their full worth, by merely harkening back to the errors of the past, to many of which, together with the men of my generation, I was a witness or party. And because I am well acquainted with the past I am able to write authoritatively about the present.

This is not a complete biography of President Trujillo, for such a work would require greater knowledge, a larger volume and a more skilled pen than mine. It is not even a full portrayal. It merely seeks to set forth the broad general outlines of the underlying elements of his make-up and essays to interpret his formidable and singular personality. It is a summary of my opinion of this brilliant and extraordinary man, arrived at by observing him from near and afar, in intimate contact and through his words and his deeds. There are direct and purely personal impressions, at times somewhat incoherent or unrelated, that do not follow the coordinated plan of a biographer or historian; however, they faithfully reflect the thought of one who sincerely believes what he states and sincerely states what he believes.

A. R. N.

January 1951

Our national motto, "God, Country and Liberty" implies an imperative duty to combat communism. The Dominican people shall cease to exist as such when they turn their back on God, when patriotism no longer inspires their actions, and when Liberty, the underlying principle of their freedom and sovereignty as a nation, is no longer the paramount ideal of all.

Rafael L. Trujillo.

Our national motto "God, Country and Liberty" implies an imperative duty to combat communism. The Dominican people shall cease to exist as such when they turn their back on God, when Christians no longer practice their devotions, and when liberty, the underlying principle of their freedom and sovereignty as a nation, is no longer the paramount ideal of all.

Rafael L. Trujillo.

BIOGRAPHICAL DATA

Generalissimo Rafael Leonidas Trujillo Molina
President of the Dominican Republic

Rafael Leonidas Trujillo Molina was born in San Cristóbal, a small town of the province of Santo Domingo in the Dominican Republic, on October twenty-fourth, 1891. He was the fourth child with whom the marriage of Don José Trujillo Valdez and Doña Julia Molina Chevalier was blessed. His immediate forebears, that is, his grandparents, were, on his father's side, Don José Trujillo Monagas and Doña Silveria Valdez; on his mother's side, Don Pedro Molina and Doña Luisa Erciná Chevalier.

His is a proud lineage. Of pure Spanish stock and endowed with a spirit of adventure and conquest, the Trujillos came to the New World during the stirring days of America's discovery and colonization. They shed their blood and contributed with their spirit to Spain's great saga, giving to the land in which they settled a strong line culminating in that stern-faced grandfather of the subject of this book who was the steadfast enemy of Cuban rebels against the Spanish crown.

The Chevalier family, coming from the France of Napoleon that astonished the world with the feats of her military leaders, stems from Joseph Chevalier, Marquis of Philbourou, who was, according to the most prevalent accounts, a member of the entourage that accompanied Leclerc, Pauline Bonaparte's husband, who came to the island in order to pacify it and to bring it under the sway of his brother-in-law, the Emperor Napoleon.

Our subject's childhood was a quiet one, conditioned by the likewise quiet atmosphere of his birthplace. His first years were spent amid the tranquility enjoyed by people living in our smaller towns. He first was taught to read and write by Doña Luisa Ercinā Chevalier, his grandmother and teacher, a lady of culture, who herself inherited the traditional culture of the French and who devoted what free time she had from household duties to the development of the minds and souls or her numerous grandchildren. Spurred on by his restless adolescence, he was sent, along with his brothers, sisters and other companions, to the village school that was conducted by Don Pablo Barinas.

Both his environment and the times curtailed his early formal education, like that of virtually all young men of his generation. The same set of circumstances soon set him to earning his own livelihood, and it was then that, under the guidance of his uncle, Don Plinio Pina Chevalier, he started as a telegraph operator. He was given an assistant's position in the village telegraph office, and from there he was sent to the main office in the nation's capital. The great vigor that would help him achieve unbounded success was already evident.

A strong desire to improve himself and his will to excel made the restless youth become his own teacher, a self-taught man who broadened his own horizons with an astonishing prescience. Working and learning in the harsh school of life, he molded his staunch character.

Contrary to the then prevalent custom, his youth did not bear the mark of romance that was so common among other young people. His attitude toward life reflected gentle and youthful skepticism. In matters of religious faith, he holds to the beliefs of his forebears, and believes that God helps those who help themselves.

This self-reliance has been characteristic of him throughout his life. He works and struggles and finds at each turn a new opportunity to rise higher. No matter the position he may hold or the service he may be rendering, he always commands respect as a leader because of his perseverance and the efficient manner in which he fulfills even the least of his duties.

Possessing an innate kindness that is an inherited trait, he is generous to a fault. However, his kind-hearted sentiments are balanced by an instinctive abhorrence of all that betrays weakness, a vice in which he will never indulge —neither for love, regard, admiration, nor pity. He is strong in facing the trials and tribulations of life, and he remains of Spartan strength in the midst of pleasure. So self-controlled is he, in fact, that at times he has succeeded in concealing painful tragedy from those nearest him and who love him most.

His vocation is one of work and action. He detests idleness as a degrading evil, and each passing hour affords to his mind some new means to exercise his faculties. He views agriculture with true affection, as the mother industry wherein all callings may be exercised. At work he oversees everything in the manner of a true captain; he has a knack for leading men in formidable creative enterprises and his is the power that impels them to carry out his system of organization and discipline.

He entered the Military Academy as a cadet and graduated with the rank of Second Lieutenant, to begin a new phase in his life. That marked the beginning of his astonishing accomplishments. The officers over him and his instructors pointed to him as one holding within himself the wherewithal to attain success. They felt that all things were possible for this curt officer whose service record was crowded with notations praising him. He gained promotions from one rank to another ahead of all his comrades at arms, and he passed through each grade with remarkable speed until he attained that of Brigadier General, Commander in Chief of the Army. This may be counted as the start of his public life.

His former classmates at the Academy regarded him with a respect beyond that which is inspired by mere comradeship, and Trujillo became an undoubted leader whose orders were universally obeyed and who had a thorough control of all his activities.

At this juncture there entered into his life a conflict —that between his career and politics. On the one hand, he was attracted by the normal rigidness of military life and it afforded him ample opportunity for his vocation as organizer; on the other hand, politics beckoned to him, despite its repulsive atmosphere of intrigue, its straining of principles ,and its devious ways that differ from the straight path of duty.

Without hesitation, resolutely, with that quickness he has shown through life, he chose the first of those two careers. His entire time was devoted to his military duties. He worked, organized, created. Under his command, the country's military institution gained prestige beyond the national frontiers. It was praised both at home and abroad. Trujillo came to be highly regarded by the members of general staffs of other countries, and well spoken of in military circles virtually everywhere in the Western Hemisphere. Military publications gave their readers his picture and spread word of his accomplishments, pointing to him as a rare man among his fellows and a comrade at arms who was able to succeed against the normal obstacles encountered in a military career as well as those springing from his particular environment.

While he was wholeheartedly engaged in getting military affairs properly organized, the country's political administration was disintegrating. Finally governmental bungling reached a critical stage and a popular revolution broke out which, though respecting the military organization, demanded a change in the civil government. Trujillo took no part in these developments; nor did he know their object and the means that were to be used. He was aware, however, of the underlying cause. That was the peak moment in his life.

Loyal to the Republic, its institutions and its Government, he withdrew to Ozama Fortress and awaited orders. The Government became confused and its orders were uncertain and hesitant. Still, he complied with those orders. For reasons that we surely cannot fathom, General Horacio Vázquez, the country's President, staged a coup d'etat against himself, appointing the leader of the revolt as Secretary of State for the Interior and Police, getting the Vice President to resign, submitting his own resignation to the National Assembly, and turning the government over to the revolutionists.

The full import of the President's action can be judged only by later generations after sufficient time has transpired. As a result of his action, General Trujillo resigned as Commander in Chief of the Army and went into retirement in his home.

The parties that had united under the banner of the revolution sought him there and proclaimed him a candidate for the office of President of the Republic. This was early in March of 1930. After his nomination was effected, the primary assemblies, in keeping with the provisions of the Constitution, elected him President on the sixteenth of May of that same year. On August sixteenth he took the oath of office before the National Assembly which had been elected at he same time as he for the 1930-1934 term.

Such is the man who is the Dominican Republic's President, and those are the events that have contributed toward making him so extraordinary a person, one of the most famous of Latin America.

RAFAEL VIDAL

Pride yourself on being a Dominican

RAFAEL L. TRUJILLO

PART ONE

THE COUNTRY

A BRIEF GEOGRAPHICAL, HISTORICAL AND POLITICAL RESUME

CHAPTER I

THE ISLAND OF SANTO DOMINGO

The island of Santo Domingo belongs to the group known as the Greater Antilles, of which it is the second in size. It is bounded on the north by the Atlantic Ocean, on the south by the Caribbean Sea, on the east by the Mona Channel that separates it from Puerto Rico, and on the west by the Wind Channel that separates it from Cuba and Jamaica.

It is situated north of the equator, across from the Gulf of Mexico, between the parallels at 19 degrees 58 minutes and 17 degrees 36 minutes, and the meridians at 68 degrees 18 minutes and 74 degrees 30 minutes, west of Greenwich. It is 410 miles long and 178 miles wide. It is 63 miles from Puerto Rico, 48 from Cuba, and 99 from Jamaica. Of the total area 19,332 square miles, that is, almost two thirds of the Island, comprise the Dominican Republic.

Its irregular coastline has countless bays, both large and small, capes and points. Through the middle of the island from west to east runs the Cordillera Central or Central Range, which contains the highest mountains in the West Indies. The highest of these is Pico Trujillo. Large rivers course through its valleys, and some are navigable in part.

Its largest lake is Lake Enriquillo, which is 34 miles long and 11 wide. Contrary to the usual case with inland bodies of water, Lake Enriquillo has salt water.

The Island's territory is shared by two republics: to the west, the Republic of Haiti; to the east, the Dominican Republic.

The climate of the Dominican Republic is generally pleasant, neither hot nor cold. In winter, overcoats are not needed; in summer, clothes can be worn with comfort. Rightly did our great poetess Salomé Ureña de Henríquez describe it thus in her immortal lines, "The Coming of Winter".

In other climes thy rigors cause
Sadly in the fields to fade
Their once happy verdant shade;
Stilled is the waters' course,
The light is fleeting, caressing breezes halted,
The flowers dead, the singing birds departed.

In my adored gentle Quisqueya*,
After autumn has spread its mantle,
In vain would one seek a sign of thee,
For on these carefree shores endlessly
Spring doth sing its gladsome canticle.

Here there is no cold of night
To fill the anguished poor with dread,
Nor must in each hearth glow a fiery light
Lending warmth to time's slow flight,
As elsewhere thou, Winter, hast demanded.

---

*Quisqueya (pronounced, approximately, kees-kay-yah) is the ancient Indian name for the island of Santo Domingo.

The mean temperature is 77º Fahrenheit. In the middle portion of the island it has gone down as far as 32ºF. In high areas, some temperate zone products grow; on the slopes and valleys, all those of the tropical zone. Rainfall is abundant. In those regions where it is scanty, President Trujillo has caused dams and irrigation canals to be built.

A third of the Republic's area is mountainous. The other two-thirds are plain. The entire island is extremely fertile. Communications are admirable; there is not a single town or village of any importance that may not be reached over a modern highway or road, a manifest result of the public works program of Trujillo's administration.

The Republic's government is essentially civil, republica, democratic and representative, in keeping with a fixed principle of its Constitution. The government is divided into the executive power, the legislative power, and the judicial power, all three independent of one another. The executive power is vested in the President of the Republic, who is elected for a period of five years. There is no Vice President. The right of succession to the office of President in case of the President's absence devolves upon the Secretary for War, Navy, and Aviation; in his absence, in turn, upon the Secretary for the Interior, Police and Communications; in the absence of both of these, upon the Secretary for the Presidency, and if all the preceding were absent, upon the Chief Justice of the Supreme Court, who would call a session of the Congress to make a definite election. In the event of his temporary absence, the President may appoint as his substitute anyone of the Secretaries who make up his Cabinet, without being bound by the rule of succession mentioned above. The President appoints the Secretaries in his Cabinet and all the administration's employees. Senate assent is required for diplomatic appointments.

The legislative power is vested in Houses: The Senate, and the Chamber of Deputies. One Senator is elected for each province, and one for the District of Santo Domingo. The deputies or representatives, one for every 60,000 inhabitants or fraction thereof exceding 30,000, with a minimum of two for each province. Elections are by means of direct vote with prior registration of the persons who are going to cast their ballot, and with minority representation whenever more than two candidates are chosen. The constitutional term is five years.

The judicial power consists of: The Supreme Court of Justice, composed of one chief justice and eight associate justices. As a court of review, the Court examines cases brought to it for determination of adherence to the law. As a court of appeals, it is the last one that may examine decisions by the appeals courts of first instance. It is the court of both first and last instance for trials of high government officials. It is the highest court in the land and exercises disciplinary authority over all members of the judicial power. The appeals courts consist of a presiding justice and four judges. There are six such appeals courts. They try appeals from decisions by the lower courts of first instance, and handle such other matters as the laws may determine. The courts of first instance are those courts where all penal, civil and commercial cases as well as appeals from the decisions of peace courts are heard.

The peace courts try simple police infractions and handle such matters as the laws may determine. There is in each court a district attorney who acts in behalf of the Attorney General; these attorneys are appointed by the executive power. Judges are chosen by secret ballot of the Senate. The land courts have charge of proceedings having to do with the land registry law and with the surveying, measurement and distribution of land. There is a superior land court and several other land courts that have original jurisdiction.

The population of the Dominican Republic is, according to the 1950 census, 2,121,083. The historian J. Marino Incháustegui has the following to say with regard to the Dominican people: "The predominant strain among the Dominican population is the creole type stemming from the intermingling of Spanish whites with the colored race that was brought to the island during the colonial era. Because of the biological evolution due to this mixture, there stand out in the Dominican type the characteristics of the white race. The Dominican people live according to the customs of European civilization." The pure black native population is 16.15%, according to the 1935 census; including foreign blacks, the total is only 19.44% of the entire population of the country. In Haiti it is 90%.

The capital of the Republic, the former city of Santo Domingo de Guzmán, is Ciudad Trujillo. This name was given to it in honor of the Benefactor of Our Country, Generalissimo Rafael L. Trujillo, who, after the terrible hurricane in 1930 that made much of it a shambles, devoted himself to its reconstruction, making it the modern, beautiful, clean and prosperous metropolis that it now is. It has 181,533 inhabitants. There are other important cities: Santiago, with a population of 56,192; San Pedro de Macorís, with 19,994; San Francisco de Macorís, with 16,152; Barahona, with 14,690; La Vega, with 14,445; Puerto Plata, with 14,419; La Romana, with 11,587; San Juan de la Maguana, with 10,099; Baní, with 10,048; Moca, with 9,739; Azua, with 7,419; Montecristi, with 4,600; and El Seibo, with 3,164 inhabitants.

The territory of the Dominican Republic consists of the District of Santo Domingo, which includes the national capital, and twenty provinces that are, in turn, subdivided into seventy-nine townships and municipal districts.

The Dominican Constitution sets forth all those rights that are inherent in the human person. Men and women enjoy identical civil and political rights. There is freedom of worship; however, the religion of the immense majority of Dominicans is the Catholic, Apostolic and Roman faith.

The Republic's principal source of wealth is its agriculture. Its main products are sugar, rice, tobacco, cacao, coffee, bananas, peanuts, plantains, yucca, beans, and vegetables. Eighty per cent of the country's population is engaged in agricultural work or in other work that is dependent upon agriculture. Livestock raising is one of the most valuable items of national productivity. Practically all of the country's exports are agricultural and livestock articles. Owing to the increased volume of that production during recent years, many of the leading imports of former years either have been produced entirely in the Republic or have diminished to an appreciable extent as such. The country produces in sufficient quantities to satisfy its own needs sugar, rice, beans, fats, beer, plantain, yucca, precious woods and lumber; moreover, it still has a considerable margin of these goods for export.

In 1946, the Republic's livestock resources were estimated at 596,679 heads of beef and dairy cattle; 142,952 horses; 546,627 hogs; 317,276 goats; 83,800 donkeys; 42,698 mules, and 29,132 sheep.

The following figures, which have been taken from the 1950 agricultural and livestock census, are self-explanatory. In 1935 cultivated land area in the Republic totalled 26,642,324 tareas, (1) while the 1950 figure was 37,737,976 tareas. In 1950, beef and dairy cattle totalled 886,981, while the figure for hogs was 1,150,222.

The Dominican Republic is not a one-crop country. President Trujillo's farm policy has consistently sought crop diversification.

The country has no monetary problem. The Dominican peso is on a par with the United States dollar.

The country's subsoil contains a wealth of minerals: iron, gold, copper, bauxite, coal, manganese, and other products. There is large-scale mining of salt and gypsum.

Dominican industry which, prior to the Trujillo Era, had hardly been launched, has grown astoundingly in the twenty years of his administration as a result of the decided protection it has enjoyed and continues to enjoy under his government. Undreamed of heights have been reached

---

(1) One **tarea** equals 600 square meters.

in recent years in the production of sugar, vegetable oils, cement, beer, cigars and cigarettes, alcohol, rum, chocolate, meat products, matches, weapons, carbonated beverages, furniture, textiles, cord, hats, footwear, wearing apparel, cheese, butter, bread, and food pastes.

In order to promote certain basic industries, President Trujillo's administration is giving priority to the development of low-cost electrical energy for industrial purposes. Plans for the future installation of electric power plants on certain rivers, especially the Bao, Nizao, Mao and Artibonito rivers, are considerably advanced, as are also those for the large-scale development of high-grade lignite deposits found in El Valle which, according to the most recent surveys, total many millions of tons.

As may be seen, the Dominican Republic has been richly endowed by a provident nature. It has a fertile soil, a healthy climate, abundant rainfall, mighty rivers, without any of the natural drawbacks existing elsewhere. Wild beasts and predatory animals are to be found only in the cages of the Zoological Garden in Ciudad Trujillo. This was explained by the Dominican poet Gastón F. Deligne in these wonderful stanzas:

QUISQUEYANA

Suavis Terra...

Whilst like is pitted against like,
The fair tropic's magic new loves awakens,
Burgeons blossoms and richest fruits,
Free from woe of winter or summer's burdens.

Whilst blood spills o'er plain and hill,
From valleys and ridges rises
A voluptuous, plaintive cooing
Uninterrupted by vulture cries.

When the warring thunder dies,
The sorrel carcass remains,
Oh burning sun! to what e'er thou will;
For this land knows not volcanoes,
Deadly fanged serpents,
Felines fierce, or carrion birds.

CHAPTER II

DECEMBER 5, 1492

Christopher Columbus discovered the island of Santo Domingo on his first voyage, on December 5, 1492. The Indians who were its aboriginal inhabitants called it Quisqueya or Haiti. Columbus, out of gratitude for Spain's aid in his prodigious undertaking, named it Hispaniola. The island was the beachhead for the colonizing of all Spanish America. Many expeditions for the discovery of new lands set out from here. It was a land of famous firsts. The first Spanish institutions in the New World were founded here. Here for the first time in America was celebrated the Holy Sacrifice of the Mass. Here is the site of the first fortress, of the first church, of the first hospital, and of the first university in the New World. Of all the lands discovered by him, Columbus loved the island of Santo Domingo most, and here, in keeping with his expressed desire, lie his earthly remains.

During the centuries of Spanish rule, the island underwent several enemy invasions —invasion by the British in 1586; systematic raids by filibusters and buccaneers; again, invasion by the British in 1655, and invasion by the French iln 1689. More than a hundred years later, in 1795, France obtained contractually complete possession over the island.

Years later the inhabitants of the eastern part of the island, led by Brigadier Don Juan Sánchez Ramírez, rose in arms and regained for the Spanish Crown that part of the island which was known as Spanish Haiti. This heroic act of loyalty by the Dominicans was neither appreciated nor understood by the Mother Country, Spain, and the colony was left to fend for itself.

It is the year 1804. The Haitian slaves in the western part of the island which was held by the French declared their independence. This blow for Haiti's freedom gave glory to the names of Toussaint, Dessalines, Petion, Henry Christophe. It is tragic indeed that these very same men were the perpetrators of savage cruelties, pillage, infamies and aggression against the Dominican people, men who blackned the pages of the island's history with misdeeds written in letters of fire and blood.

An unenviable glory is that of those great men whose renown and whose place in history are based on the conquest and annihilation of other peoples in a blind and selfish service of their own country's ambition, bringing to other lands tragedy, desolation, and death.

The name of Attila, the terrible conqueror who devastated Europe, echoes down through history to this day. Likewise that of Julius Caesar, the lord of both glory and oppression. So with Napoleon's name on the other side of the Pyrennees, and Bismarck's beyond the Rhine!

The birth of Haiti as an independent nation aroused in the minds of her statesmen the idea of extending their rule over the entire island, which they always viewed as one and indivisible, under Haiti's flag.

In 1821, fearing renewed invasion by the Haitians, and in view of Spain's neglect of Santo Domingo, Núñez de Cáceres proclaimed the latter's independence, declaring it an autonomous state under the protection of Grand Colombia. He sought Bolivar's aid urgently. The Liberator, who had not yet completed his great mission, was either unable or unwilling —possibly out of gratitude toward Haiti for its help in his great undertaking— to lend protection to the newborn nation that had cast off Spanish rule. The inevitable happened. The Haitians invaded the Spanish part of the island. The disgraceful Haitian rule lasted twenty-two years. The darkest shadows engulfed our land. Our religion was profaned, our women violated, our most sacred institutions trampled, our most ancient traditions mocked, and our customs corrupted. Our best families, that is, those holding our wealth and our culture, fled in terror to other lands. The ruthless Haitian occupation brought long, tragic years of abuse, crimes without number and silent martyrdom.

On February 27, 1844 the Dominican people cast off the shackles of bondage and launched their national freedom. The glorious movement was led by the three great Founding Fathers of our country: Juan Pablo Duarte, its intellectual author; Francisco del Rosario Sánchez, the man of action, and Ramón Matías Mella, who sparked the movement.

In the ranks of those who fought heroically beside these great champions of freedom, each in his own manner, were: the foremost of them all, the valiant General Pedro Santana, without whose sword victory might never have been achieved, José Joaquín Puello, Felipe Alfáu, Eduardo Abréu, Pedro Alejandrino Pina, Jacinto de la Concha, Wenceslao de la Concha, Félix María Ruiz, José Ma. Serra, Benito González, Remigio del Castillo, Nepomuceno Ravelo, Juan Isidro Pérez, Pedro Ramón de Mena, Manuel Jiménez, Vicente Celestino Duarte, Trinidad Sánchez, José Ma. Imbert, Antonio Duvergé, Fernando Valerio, Pepillo Salcedo, Pedro de Castro y Castro, Mariano Echavarría, José Ma. Cabral, Esteban Roca, Eusebio Pereyra, Francisco Sosa, Valentín Alcántara and many others whose deeds and heroism are recorded in history.

General Pedro Santana was elected by the Congress as the Republic's first President; he was chosen for two consecutive four-year terms. As a result of differences that arose between him and the Congress, General Santana resigned the office in 1848. General Manuel Jiménez, his Minister of War, was then chosen to succeed him. Some months later the government of President Jiménez was in turn overthrown by the triumphant troops of General Santana who, after having won resounding victories over the Haitians, revolted against the former's government. At Santana's suggestion, the Congress then elected Colonel Buenaventura Báez as President.

Báez' rise to power ushered in the protracted, shameful and humiliating efforts of successive Dominican administrations to obtain the establishment of a foreign protectorate. Báez looked to France, Britain or the United States to create a protectorate, while Santana sought annexation by Spain. Today, when viewed solely from the standpoint of the selfish political interests that may have guided each, their questionable negotiations may be regarded as shameful. With detachment, after these many years, one must admit, however, that the profound desire for annexation was due to the latent fear then prevalent of a new Haitian occupation as well as to lack of faith in our ability to repel the same permanently with our own forces.

In February of 1853, General Santana took the oath of office for a second time as President. A few months later, increasing hostility toward his government led him to resign. The election went to General Manuel de Regla Mota, a weak leader who, for some reason, failed to rise to the occasion and resigned as President. General Buenaventura Báez was then elected for a second time.

At that time, the Dominican people were no longer beset by the nightmare of Haitian invasion with its attendant atrocities. It would seem that, aided by the existing favorable circumstances, the government would undertake the important task of organization and progress that the country's interests demanded. Things turned out quite otherwise. The economic chaos and political persecutions that marked Báez' second administration caused widespread discontent. As a result, revolution again broke out and General Santana became President once more.

During his new term of office, General Santana, who had long desired and planned the annexation of the Republic by Spain, considering the time ripe, put his carefully prepared plan into execution. Unbeknownst to the people, secret negotiations were initiated. Santana's power and the blind political passion of his partisans took care of the rest. When the people became aware of what had been going on it was too late. It was a terrible, unforgivable mistake that forever tarnished the laurels of the valiant Liberator. The Spanish Crown rewarded General Santana's ignominious action with the title of Marquis of Las Carreras and an appointment as Captain General as well as Governor of the new colony.

General Santana remains an enigmatic figure in history; of reckless bravery, haughty and brusque in manner but, at the same time, receptive to counsel and intrigue; ambitious yet selfless; lacking in formal education but endowed with the soldierly spirit of the Creoles developed to the maximum. He was our real military genius in the struggle against the Haitians. Unfortunate blots stand against his record: the Spanish annexation; the execution of Trinidad Sánchez; the martyrdom of Francisco del Rosario Sánchez; the imprisonment of the Puellos and Dugergé. These, however, do not eclipse his brilliant military deeds that brought about our decisive victory over Haiti, and to which our nation owes its existence

The best excuse for his most serious mistake, the annexation, is that at heart Santana was more a Spaniard than a Dominican. His fierce hatred for Haiti, that so often led him to heroic actions, was more a racial hatred than burning indignation caused by outraged patriotism. Santana was sincerely convinced that the Dominican Republic, Spain's helpless daughter, could not thrive and maintain itself in a sound condition save under Spain's motherly tutelage. He later came to see and to understand his fatal error. But it was too late. He must have died with an unmitigted sorrow in his soul.

It has been during the Trujillo Era that General Santana has been first accorded the justice that is his due in history. Formerly, the very mention of his hated name aroused patriotic indignation. School children were confused, their minds filled with grievances and poisoned with the hatred that his political enemies bore Santana and which the textbooks propagated. The stigma of treason seemed inextricably linked to his name, and his unequalled heroism in battle, his inflexible attitude toward the Haitian invaders, his legendary valor that was never found wanting in the face of peril and responsibility gradually became dimmed and eventually forgotten amid the chorus of general opprobrium.

Trujillo, however, has sponsored an unbiased appraisal, in books and in the public press, of General Santana as a historic figure. Betokening official recognition of his broad military vision and admirable strategy, Trujillo ordered that there be held, on the very site where the famous battle of Las Carreras was fought, a full-scale reenactment, under his personal direction, of that decisive battle that placed the nation's flag on high, where it remains today for all to see. Were it not for the Spartan bravery and the great strategic ability that General Pedro Santana displayed in that battle, it is quite likely that by now the entire population of this Island would be Haitian.

Two years were passed under Spanish rule. On August 16, 1863, a group of gallant patriots met in Capotillo and proclaimed the restoration of the Dominican Republic. The annals of the ensuing campaign for liberation record the heroic names of Benito Monción, José Cabrera, Juan A. Polanco, Santiago Rodríguez, Pedro A. Pimentel, Olegario Tenares, Eusebio Manzueta, Eusebio Pereyra, Benigno F. de Rojas, and the greatest hero of them all, General Gregorio Luperón.

During the War for Restoration the office of President was held by General Gaspar Polanco, Benigno F. de Rojas, General Pedro A. Pimentel, and General Pepillo Salcedo, who was assassinated. The latter was replaced by General Gaspar Polanco, an accomplice in the assassination, who, in turn, was overthrown shortly thereafter by the forces of his former comrades in arms, General Benito Monción and General Pedro A. Pimentel. The next President was Benigno F. de Rojas; he, in turn, was replaced, as a result of sordid political scheming, by General Pedro A. Pimentel.

After General Pimentel, General José Ma. Cabral, hero of the battles of Santomé and La Canela, was elected. Shortly thereafter, a revolt overthrew General Cabral's government, which was supported by the Blue Party, and for a third time the office fell to General Buenaventura Báez, head of the Red Party. The following year a fresh revolt forced President Báez to seek asylum in the French Consulate, and General José Ma. Cabral became President anew. It was not long before another revolution overthrew him and made General Buenaventura Báez chief executive for a fourth time.

Báez' new term of office is noteworthy for two nefarious events. A loan contracted by his administration with the firm of Hartmont and Company of London initiated the long, painful and humiliating experience of our nation with foreign debts, and two treaties were concluded with the United States Government, one leasing Samaná Bay and the other providing for the Republic's annexation by the United States. Neither of these treaties were put into effect because they were never ratified by the United States Senate.

These events were the basis, or, rather, the pretext for the Red and Blue parties uniting against President Báez, and a subversive movement began in Puerto Plata. The leader of the popular movement, General Ignacio María González, a man of great social prestige and polished manners, was elected President of the Republic. In 1876 political circumstances compelled General González' resignation, and the man then elected for the highest office in the land was the peerless patriot, Ulises Francisco Espaillat. His administration brought a very brief interval in which probity and patriotism reigned. A revolution led by General Ignacio María González deposed Espaillat's civic government, and General González once more became President. But he was out in the twinkling of an eye. Following the quick overthrow wrought by Báez' supporters, the latter was called, in keeping with what was now a custom, to become President; but another revolution, led by General Cesáreo Guillermo, forced Báez' resignation.

General Buenaventura Báez was President of the Republic on five different occasions. Whatever services he rendered his country seem to have been inspired by personal ambition or interest. Intelligent, well educated, astute —he was an able politician who succeeded in arousing enthusiasm and loyalty among his supporters. His greatest crime, the abortive annexation by the United States, is inexcusable. Himself a member of the colored race, one cannot understand that he should want his country to be ruled by a nation that had maintained slavery until a short time before and that held his race in deep contempt. He had been Deputy for Azua in the Haitian Congress. At the time of the Spanish annexation, he accepted the rank of Field Marshal of Spain given to him by the Spaniards. It would appear that in his hands the nation was a mere tool for ambition.

After Báez' resignation, General Ignacio María González was designated President for a third time. His term lasted three months, for another revolution led by the same General Cesáreo Guillermo placed in that office Jacinto de Castro, an inocuous but well-meaning man who soon resigned. Thereupon General Cesáreo Guillermo was elected. But a new uprising overthrew the daring and ambitious General Guillermo and carried General Gregorio Luperón to the highest office in the land. General Luperón did not want to be President, and, giving him the full support of his immense prestige, he had Fernando Arturo de Meriño, a clergyman and our most eloquent orator, and likewise an outstanding figure in politics as well as in the Church, made President. At the end of his two-year term, General Ulises Heureaux was elected. It is noteworthy that this was the first time that a change of administration was effected by lawful and pacific means. Two years later, wily General Heureaux sponsored the candidacy of Francisco Gregorio Billini, a distinguished citizen. The political demands of the day proved too harsh for the gentle President Billini, who turned the office over to the Vice President, General Alejandro Woss y Gil. For the following term General Heureaux was elected. By means of successive reelections General Heureaux was President from that year, 1887, up until July 26, 1899, when he was assassinated in the city of Moca by a group of conspirators under Ramón Cáceres and Horacio Vásquez.

General Heureaux's long tenure of office is noteworthy, particularly during its latter part, for the implacable fury with which he persecuted his rivals; for his ill-advised financial transactions that raised the foreign debt to more than $20,000,000, and for his dishonest negotiations with Haiti regarding the boundary between the two countries. On the positive side of the ledger, we find in his favor, as progressive measures, only the construction of the narrow-gauge railway from Puerto Plata to Santiago, the construction of the bridge over the Ozama River, and a relative organization of the National Army, exceedingly meager works that can be counted with less than the fingers of one hand. His mailed fist brought domestic tranquility, but Heureaux lacked either the wisdom or the ability to translate it into constructive works and a sound administration.

A cool appraisal reveals President Heureaux as an interesting character indeed. He was despised by his enemies unto death; his friends loved him even beyond the grave. Such was the natural result of a system of government that, generations later, would be imitated by Mussolini: "The best for our friends; the worst for our enemies." He was at once affable and bloodthirsty, sensual and cruel

Extremely vengeful, he was the while capable of waiting aloofly, with all quiet, year after year, nursing grudges, to later avenge an offense or even a score. A dagger concealed under silks. A poisoned perfume. Such was General Heureaux. He lived bravely and died bravely, ever facing all perils. He was very fine of manner, very astute, very hard working; but he was also ignorant, to such an extent that he sincerely believed that paper currency could be issued against the hangman's noose, as though it were gold. Extremely wily, his political sagacity far outclassed that of his contemporaries, and his was the rare asset, so priceless to a politician, of having an intimate knowledge of men. His treatment of them was in keeping with the idea that he had of each individual. Respectful toward those who deserved respect, he was cynically flattering and cruel with those capable of betraying him. In the War of Restoration his victorious sword wrote brilliant pages of history. In our civil struggles, his bravery and his cruelty were equal. A wretched administrator, his twenty years of office led the country into complete bankruptcy.

*

* *

Upon General Heureaux's death, after a brief interval under former Vice President Figuereo, General Horacio Vásquez formed a provisional government. In the ensuing elections Don Juan Isidro Jiménez was elected President of the Republic and General Vásquez as Vice President. President Jiménez' administration tried in vain to straighten public finances and to bring order out of chaos.

The avarice of the Santo Domingo Improvement Company, an American corporation, on the one hand, and, on the other, the restless political ambitions of his adversaries, and, above all, his own lack of foresight, prevented it.

Two years after the inaugural of the Jiménez-Vásquez administration, Vice President Vásquez turned against the President and forced his resignation. Vásquez immediately formed a provisioinal government. It was this de facto government that, as a result of the active efforts of American Minister Powell, recognized, without requiring any prior accounting, as a debt of the Republic, the amount of $4,000,000 owed to the Improvement Company. Not to be outdone, Minister Powell tendered diplomatic recognition to Vásquez' provisional government. Eleven months later, the government was overthrown by a daring coup executed by the prisoners in the Torre del Homenaje in the nation's capital, led by General Perico Pepín, on March 23, 1903. Upon the downfall of Vásquez, General Alejandro Woss y Gil took over the government and it was during the latter's administration that an arbitral award was granted in the United States against the Republic and in favor of the Improvement Company. Under the award the Company was given control over several of the country's customhouses.

A revolution led by General Carlos F. Morales overthrew Woss y Gil and made Morales President.

During Morales' administration, at the suggestion of President Theodore Roosevelt, the first convention between the Dominican Republic and the United States was concluded; the convention failed, however, to obtain ratification in the United States Senate.

President Morales bent every effort toward setting the country on the right track but the unstable and difficult political situation prevailing within his own administration brought about his early downfall. Upon his resignation the Vice President, General Ramón Cáceres, assumed the office of President.

General Cáceres' government decisively crushed revolutionary outbreaks along the turbulent North. During his administration the convention between the Dominican Republic and the United States was ratified. His administration sought tenaciously to maintain order in public finances and got the construction of certain public works under way. On November 19, 1911, he was assassinated by revolutionary conspirators whose principal leaders were General Luis Tejera and Luis Felipe Vidal.

In the midst of the ensuing chaos, the National Congress, acting under pressure brought to bear by the armed forces of the Republic, elected as President Eladio Victoria, an uncle of General Alfredo Victoria, the chief of staff of the Army and the strong man of the hour, who lacked the legal age to become President. The armed rebellion went on, however, President Victoria being finally forced to resign. As a result of United States mediation, the National Congress chose as Victoria's successor Archbishop Monsignor Adolfo Nouel. The benevolent prelate was able to withstand only for a few months the savage onslaughts of the contending political parties. Quitting the capital, ill and discouraged, he resigned the office.

The Congress then elected General José Bordas Valdez. The opposition was not long in rising in arms. The revolution spread. The United States again intervened, this time openly, forcing the leaders of the political parties to chose a President, under threat that, should they not do so, President Woodrow Wilson would do it himself. Given that choice, the parties came to an agreement and chose Dr. Ramón Báez, a prominent citizen, as President. Elections were held under United States supervision, and for a second time Juan Isidro Jiménez was elected. Shortly after he took office, his Secretary of War, General Desiderio Arias, rose against him with the help of the Army. Indescribable chaos reigned. Troops were landed from American warships anchored ouside the capital. President Jiménez resigned. In July, 1916 the National Congress, that was especially convoked, elected to succeed Jiménez, Dr. Francisco Henríquez y Carvajal, a man of science who had been absent from the country for many years. The United States refused to grant recognition to this government and, invoking the convention, deprived it of the customs revenues. In view of the conflict between authorities and without an agreement having been reached with the Henríquez y Carvajal administration, the United States decided upon the most direct though the most drastic solution —military occupation. On November 21, 1916 a proclamation to that effect was issued by Captain H. S. Knapp.

The military occupation by the United States proved a harsh and bitter lesson that should have been taken to heart by those Dominicans to whom the nation's government later was entrusted.

The Military Occupation was decreed under the pretext that the Republic had violated the Convention of 1907 by increasing its public debt. Under the Military Government, however, that public debt was increased. The most rigid censorship was imposed; rutheless military action stamped out all resistance. So extreme were the measures adopted by some American officers during the Occupation, that Dominican complaints were heard even in the halls of the United States Senate which ordered an investigation and appointed a committee of its members to visit the country. On the credit side of the Military Government's ledger there are to be found only the construction of the Central Highway, the confiscation of the citizenry's firearms, and a greater progress achieved in public education.

After six years had passed and by virtue of the Plan conceived by Francisco J. Peynado, which was accepted by Charles Evans Hughes, Secretary of State of the United States, in the drafting of which the heads of the Dominican parties and other prominent citizens collaborated, the gradual withdrawal of the occupation forces got under way, and, by a strange whim of fortune, Juan B. Vicini Burgos, a wealthy man who had no party affiliation, was elected Provisional President. Vicini Burgos fulfilled his mission ably. His administration was honest, and he was impartial. His lack of political bias was made manifest by the contempt with which he treated all parties alike.

In keeping with the provisions of the Hughes-Peynado Plan, at the end of two years general elections were held. General Horacio Vásquez won those elections. General Vásquez' administration proved disappointing, however, and he proved unmindful of the bitter experiences under the Military Occupation. Public monies were misappropriated; political bossim and splinter parties were encouraged; large loans were contracted and although public works were carried out, their value fell far short of the $80,000,000 that his administration collected in revenues. In February of 1930 a popular revolution in which hardly a shot was fired put an end to his government.

Before sending to the Congress his own resignation together with that of Vice President Alfonseca, President Vásquez appointed the head of the revolution itself, Rafael Estrella Ureña, as Secretary of the Interior and Police, and the latter thus became President in accordance with provisions of the Constitution.

This was followed by a period of indecision or, rather, of confusion among the old political parties. All were dumbfounded; something unprecedented was happening. People no longer had any faith in them. Their leaders stood discredited. Their promises met with skepticism. And the people, from the depths of their disillusionment, turned hopefully to the only man in whom they could trust at that stage, Rafael Leonidas Trujillo. Swept by the overwhelming wave of popular enthusiasm, all the parties opposing Vásquez discarded their own leaders, joined forces, and rallied around Trujillo, nominating him as their candidate. To oppose his candidacy the former President's partisans presented their own nominee. It was a futile effort, the weak fluttering of a bird already mortally wounded through its own fault. The irresistible tide of Trujillo's popularity grew ever greater.

In an underhanded and subtle manner the opposition sought to obstruct the electoral process after it was already under way, claiming that a lack of electoral boards made it materially impossible to hold the elections as provided for in the Constitution. The Central Electoral Board set about appointing the local boards deliberately in so slow, lackadaisical and difficult a fashion that it almost succeeded in its plan that May 16, 1930 be reached without the electoral boards for the balloting. Estrella Ureña's administration would thus become a **de facto** government. The Constitution was to be flouted, and with it all the institutions of the State, ushering in a new era of government with no fixed term and with dictatorial powers, under Estrella Ureña, the revolution's leader, who would be President and would order elections to be held at some arbitrary date, thus frustrating the will of the people, an overwhelming majority of whom favored Trujillo's candidacy.

Upon his return from a triumphant campaign trip through the Cibao region, Trujillo was warned of this underhanded scheme. Thereupon the necessary steps were taken to meet the danger. The members of the Central Electoral Board submitted their resignations. The Senate appointed new judges to the Central Electoral Board. The Board, in one sweeping decree, confirmed the same members of the Electoral Boards who had presided over the preceding general elections, as there was no longer time for any other measure. The sly scheme for a **de facto** government fell through. The general elections were held, their outcome was approved by the existing National Congress, as provided by law, and the election went to gallant General Rafael L. Trujillo Molina, who had been destined by an unscrutable Providence to change completely the course of history and to effect a thorough transformation of his country.

More than fifty Presidents in eighty-six years of independent life! More than thirty revolutions —bloodshed, plunder, arson, the destruction of wealth, the stifling of all progress, and national stagnation!

We have presented the frightful panorama of our history in these few words. A tragic picture of desolation, indeed, but a true and accurate one.

Now we turn to a new page, for that chaos is a thing of the past.

An empty life without great affections,
without awareness of the eternal truths,
is not worth living.

María Martínez de Trujillo

PART TWO

TRUJILLO, THE MAN

CHAPTER III

THE FAMILY TREE

As is known, two of Trujillo's outstanding forebears were a distinguished Spanish Army officer and a French marquis, that is, two **conquistadores**, complete even to sword, cape and the cross over their hearts. (1).

Among noteworthy traits of his immediate forebears, we find the warm and engaging cordial manner of his father and the sweet and gentle goodness of his mother, in whose heart are harbored all the womanly virtues. His Dominican grandmother endowed him with skill, caution and political intuition; from his Spanish grandfather he inherited courage, vitality and self-discipline. The happy combination of these forces produced President Trujillo, that uncommon, enigmatic and splendid man.

---

(1) Reporting a public talk delivered by the noted Spanish scholar García Sanchiz in San Cristóbal, the newspaper "La Nación" published the following:

"The noble Spanish lineage of his surnames, Trujillo and Molina. **Trujillo**, a name from famous Extremadura, as those of the great **conquistadores** Cortés and Pizarro as well as those of others who brought the vastness of Castile to American shores.

Molina, the name that alongside that of Vizcaya is borne by the Spanish kings, denoting the only **señoríos** or suzerainties over which they were lords, and the illustrious surname of the Regent Doña María de Molina; also the name of other famous Spaniards, including the great "Lagartijo", whose real name was Rafael Molina and who was called affectionately caliph of his native Córdoba.

His paternal grandfather was Don José Trujillo y Monagas, a Spanish officer, who distinguished himself in Havana because of his wisdom and devotion in the fulfillment of his duties as Chief of Police of that famous city. Only exceptionally qualified individuals enjoying great prestige were given that office.(2) His grandmother on the same side was Doña Silveria Valdez, who was related to some of the most distinguished families of San Cristóbal and Baní and was a very active, intelligent and gallant lady.

His father was Don José Trujillo Valdez, a San Cristóbal landowner and a local, social and political leader there. He was a hardworking, helpful, generous, and kind-hearted man. He lived to enjoy his son's triumphs and co-operated with enthusiasm, successfully, in the latter's work for national reconstruction. He served in the National Congress. He is remembered with true veneration in Baní, his birthplace. President Trujillo's mother is Doña Julia Molina Trujillo Valdez. She was born in San Cristóbal with its cool climate and warm hospitality, green and fertile fields, rich untilled lands; small and glistening frame houses, painted red, yellow or pink, with thatched roofs; wide streets, velvety pastures where cattle thrived, a picture of pastoral beauty worthy of the brush of a Corot

---

(2) In his biography of Don José Trujillo y Monagas, published in Barcelona in 1882, Carlos Urrutia states the following: "He was endowed with superabundant will power, a strong character, vitality, sagacity, courage and other virtues. He was a persevering and inflexible man". He was decorated several times by the King of Spain for heroism in combat and distinguished services. The reader might well think that this is a description of the grandson rather than of his forebear.

and the verses of a Horace, when it was a pleasant small town and not the thriving center it is today. (3)

In those days San Cristóbal was without social centers and sports clubs, and the young set would find entertainment by gathering in the statelier homes, generally those of Doña Erciná Chevalier, José Dolores Pereyra and Lowes-ki Montás, or else a picturesque group would go on horse-back, to the accompaniment of music, laughter and singing, to the beautiful waterfall of La Toma, or Pomier Caves; on these outings, the ladies, adorned with perfumed flowers in their tresses, bedecked with coral necklaces and Madras kerchiefs over their shoulders, rode as skilfully as the men. Generally the youth from socially prominent families of the capital city would join in these simple and wholesome gatherings in San Cristóbal. At that time the town's most distinguished social group included the Misses Julia Molina, Altagracia Sánchez, Aurelia de León, Anita Saladín, Atalia and Tescelina Valdez, Anita and Tona Franco, Manuela and Ramona La Paix, Mercedes and Rafaela Montás, Bernard, Agueda and Efigenia Renvill, Palmira and Antonia Leger, Anita, Mercedes, Rosa and Niña Pereyra; and of the opposite sex, José Trujillo Valdez,

---

(3) Twenty years after President Trujillo's election in 1930, San Cristóbal has become a modern, beautiful and cultured city. It boasts new public buildings, magnificent schools, a theatre, a splendid club, and an agricultural institute. Its wide and spotless streets, its broad avenues, its hospitals and sanatoriums, comportable hotels and casinos, its drives, gardens, swimming facilities, and, in fine, all its astounding progress are owned to Trujillo. San Cristóbal, today called the **Ciudad Benemérita** or noble city, was the site of the adoption of the first Constitution of the Republic, and is the birthplace of Trujillo himself, the country's greatest statesman.

Juan Pablo Pina, Julio Pereyra, Bilito Leger, Ernesto Molina, Fellé and Régulo de León, Alberto Vargas, Manuel Piña, Lucas Díaz, Leonidas Saladín, Marcos and José Uribe, Julián and Pablo Barinas, and Jesús Nivar.

Among the ladies, Julia Molina stood out for her striking beauty, her large and lovely dark eyes, her silken hair and her patrician bearing, as well as for her culture, shining virtue and innate goodness. An expert horsewoman, she mastered the most fiery steeds; a graceful dancer, she was especially sought out at balls; a daring and skillfull swimmer, she once saved the life of her friend Tescelina Valdez; generous and charitable, her gentle hands were ever quick to succor the needy. In her carefree youth, hardly could she have imagined that she was destined to be, through her blissful union with José Trujillo Valdez, the mother of her country's most famous statesman who is the architect of its greatness. From her loving hands he received the iron moral fibre and the intellectual brilliance that lighted his path to win the nation's admiration, affection and gratitude.

A warmly affectionate son even to the minutest detail, President Trujillo's love for his mother, evinced at every turn by a respectful and attentive solicitude, knows no bounds. A worthy son of such a paragon of the womanly virtues! Her charitable deeds, quietly performed, are without number. She treasures the memory of her loving husband, Don José Trujillo Valdez, priding herself in his fame as a progressive legislator, a noble and selfless gentleman, and that of her son Aníbal, gone from this life all too soon in 1948, in the fullness of youth and vigor; like Bayard's, his was a romantic, valorous spirit.

The Trujillo-Molina union was blessed with numerous offspring —Virgilio, Marina, Rafael Leonidas, Aníbal Julio, José Arismendí (1), Romeo, Julieta, Nieves Luisa, Japonesa, Pedro and Héctor Bienvenido.

---

(1) Colonel José Arismendi Trujillo Molina, founder and owner of "La Voz Dominicana" has been, as the other members of the family, a loyal, active and efficient supporter of President Trujillo. He has aided him intelligently and enthusiastically in politics, in the country's cultural development, and in its astounding social and commercial progress. His powerful broadcasting station, which, by dint of great financial sacrifice, he has succeeded in making one of the best in Latin America, and whose programs have featured the most famous stars as well as leaders in the sciences, literature and diplomacy, has been a decisive factor in disseminating knowledge throughout the world as to Trujillo's gigantic achievements for his country.

CHAPTER IV

1937

Throughout the years, whether as Generalissimo in 1937, General in 1927 or Lieutenant in 1917, Trujillo has remained one and the same. Essentially, time has wrought no change in the man himself.

Though it has unfolded in so dazzling a manner, his life is without sharp contrasts or ups and downs. It has followed a consistent development as befits one whose every thought and action have been in keeping with so high a mission.

In the mature man are to be found the same basic traits that distinguished him in his youth: an abiding sense of responsibility, patriotism, intelligence, courage, and, above all, a thirst for glory and a passion for outdoing his own achievements. A nature so rarely endowed calls for just such a splendid development, a prodigious fulfillment of the capabilities of one predestined by Divine Providence to accomplish a mission at once singular, of transcendental importance, and superhuman in scope: the complete regeneration of a nation, involving both its reconstruction in the material order and its moral rehabilitation. Such a task unquestionably calls for a genius and a hero whom we may call a veritable superman, if it is to be performed without interruptions due to failures and successfully carried out so as to achieve definitive and lasting results.

Among the traits we have mentioned are to be found a thoroughly clear mind; an unfailing memory, particularly for those things that others are prone to forget; a penetrating, sagacious, analytical and profound type of intelligence, quick to grasp and lighting-like in its decisions; an iron will, disciplined and firm, equal to any effort, untiring amid the most arduous tasks, and a source of unfailing patience when necessary; psychologically, at once complex and uncomplicated, multi-faceted, and receptive; resilient and tempered as fine steel; proud as the eagle, undaunted by any height; arrogant toward the arrogant; gentle and protecting toward the humble. Being implacable, yet gentle; a realist, yet a dreamer; audacious, yet patient; quick, yet calm, withal, his self-control has made Trujillo the arbitrer of his own life wherein all actions, even those requiring the greatest audacity, are performed with calm deliberation. A man who sometimes has proven himself unaware of his own strength and of the full power of his personality, he is frank to the point of bluntness. His words oftentimes may sound harsh, but he is always clear and to the point. A man of contrasts, whatever may seem at first a contradiction turns out to be, when viewed in its geometrical whole, entirely in keeping with the four cardinal points in his make-up —patriotism, thirst for glory, valor and intelligence, all tying in together.

His friendship, though generous, is never depreciated by exaggeration; though severe in meting out punishment, he is devoid of cruelty. Never wittingly unjust, he is at times unyielding, and certainly always sincere. His pragmatism and apparent skepticism notwithstanding, his idealism is sensitive and impassioned, more so than one might suspect in a person so unfathomable and cautious as well as withdrawn and aloof. He is relentless with traitors, and yet tender in his affections. He is a friend to reckon with, and an enemy to reckon with. Profoundly human; every inch a man. And he is more —a leader.

Trujillo is a clear example of the fact that the great men of history can only be explained by their very contradictions. They are better subjects for paradox than for hyperbole. Their very psychological complexity makes them understandable. Diverse tonal values and seemingly discordant notes make, in their case, a coherent whole. In each, all his multiple facets reflect light from one same source.

President Trujillo has for his friends a devotion that is rarely to be found in great political leaders, who as a rule grow indifferent due to the harshness of politics, with its attendant intimate contact with men that brings bitter disillusionment because of the viler side of humanity that is so often exposed, revealing the absence of gratitude and kindness.

Geniuses act independently of norms. Only average men leading average lives conform to the rules of general mediocrity. Mediocre men adapt themselves to universal standards, that is, to a single, selfsame measure. The great men of history are those who tower over the mass.

Trujillo's greatness consists, however, not only in towering over his fellows, but also in the encompassing nature of his achievements. His is not the loftiness of a granite column, but rather that of a majestic mountain range.

CHAPTER V

PORTRAIT STUDY

His oval face and gentle features are, characteristically, highly expressive, as much in moments of anger as when a cordial smile shows itself. His eyes, full of expression, are radiant and of an indefinable color. They are penetrating, analytical, and probing. At times they have a razor-sharp harshness; at other times they glow with the warmth of affection. Aloof and reserved, enigmatic Trujillo is a serious thinker whose thoughts no one can divine and for whom gaiety is but a passing whim. Myriad legends have been spun around him, doubtless owing to his unscrutability.

Though normally his eyes reveal his soul, when he is engaged in deep thought they become enigmatic, with a far-away look. This happens often. Sometimes his abstraction lasts a long while, and on those occasions his eyes are as if probing some event or some person clearly fixed in his imagination and they take on a sombre hue. The light seems gone from them, as though to illuminate the inner recesses of his mind.

His face is rather finely drawn; his nose would reveal a strong character. His clipped, silvery-gray mustache, matching the color of his hair, is in marked contrast with a decided youthfulness about his face. Arched eyebrows betray a certain haughtiness, obduracy and strength. His high forehead befits his noble thoughts.

His laughter is hearty and contagious. It is readily forthcoming whenever something strikes him as humorous, and its resonance finds an echo among his hearers.

He is very neat about his person. His wardrobe reveals care and good taste, combining simplicity with elegance, and might well be envied by a prince. His collection of neckties is famous. The best tailors in New York, London and Paris fashion his clothes.

His manner is urbane, and is readily adapted to any situation. On occasions he is gallant and attentive; when among simple countryfolk he is plain and jovial. Either in uniform or in mufti, he would be an immediate success at any gathering of society in Europe or in the United States.

Women delight him. He is unfailingly gallant, attentive and considerate toward them. He enjoys being in their company. He is genuinely impressed by femenine beauty. Handsome and of striking bearing, it hardly need be added that his enormous popularity with the fair sex stems from something other than politics. When he makes his way through enthusiastic crowds, many a look of admiration from feminine eyes is sent his way for the man he is, independenlty of his being a national hero.

Well built, soldierly without being pompous, of average height, the President cuts a good figure. His winning ways not only assure receptiveness on the part of his hearers, but are such as to influence even his enemies.

On two occasions, leaving behind his astonished aides and at grave risk of his life, he penetrated alone into an enemy guerrilla encampment. His personal magnetism and his power of persuasion won the day without need of using any weapons. The guerrillas laid their arms down.

Another of President Trujillo's remarkable assets is his ability as a conversationalist. Spiced with a mordant sense of humor, his words come in a free and easy manner. Neither pompous nor stuffy— in the company of intimates he does not stand on protocol— his joviality rises to the surface effortlessly, in a natural and spontaneous manner, and the arguments he puts forth in the cordial tones of camaraderie usually carry the day. When he speaks in public his remarks are punctuated by appropriate gestures and delivered in a tone that, though gentle, has a ring of command, and the conviction underlying his every word moves his audience to genuine enthusiasm.

He is free of fetishes and quirks. He likes animals but not exaggeratedly. Nor is he exaggeratedly fond of hunting and fishing; neither can he be called a sports fan. Unlike Franklin Delano Roosevelt, he is not a philatelist; nor does he collect coins as did the late King Victor Emmanuele; nor lions and tigers as did Goering and Juan Vicente Gómez of Venezuela. His sole hobby is horses, which he rides masterfully. He is uninitiated in games of chance. He is frugal and methodical in his eating habits, and, despite his ability to withstand the intoxicating effects of alcohol, he is a light drinker. He is a non-smoker. As Rubén Darío would have expressed it, he is "a veritable dynamo". Afoot or on horseback, he makes long journeys without tiring. His vigor and agility are truly amazing. In travels over rough mountains his endurance has been greater than that of any of the aides accompanying him.

Although from youth he has been a professional soldier, even above that vocation his true and favorite calling has been agriculture and livestock raising, in keeping with the creative talent with which Providence endowed him.

His first employment upon leaving school in order to help his parents was as a telegraph operator, which happened to be the occupation of two of his uncles, on his mother's side, Teódulo and Plinio B. Pina Chevalier. But his love of nature would not be denied, and he was drawn at an early age to the fields. Later he enrolled in the School of Agriculture that operated for some time in San Cristóbal. However, the need to earn a livelihood led him into other avenues. His iron character and his strong will were gradually forged on the hard anvil of life. He enlisted in the army and subsequently enrolled in the Training Center at Jaina. From that moment the bright star of his destiny began its rise.

Since 1930 all his free time from the cares of government has been devoted to developing large estates where the products of the soil yield a rich harvest and cattle is improved through breeding. His clean, modern and sanitary barns are the equal of those to be found in the most up to date model farm in the United States, and they are for him a source of unfailing delight. He derives genuine enjoyment from the gentle loving of the cattle, their restlessness, the pungent odor of newly ploughed land, the early morning air in the fields wafting the fragrance of freshly opened flowers, the cool fog drifting from distant hills over the pastures, and the green fields swaying in the soft morning breeze. Many of his animals he calls by name and strokes affectionately. There is no denying that Trujillo is happier in the country than in the city. He is drawn by nature. A green forest, a swift flowing stream, or a towering hill enchant him.

Of the fine arts he prefers music and poetry, although he has not delved deeply into either. As a youth, however, he wrote verses. In this connection, I recall that once, at an intimate gathering, he challenged Osvaldo Bazil, the poet, to recite some verses. (1) Poems by Rubén Darío, Nervo, and Apolinar Perdomo were recited. Bazil recited some of his own, and Trujillo a sonnet he had written in his youth. He reaped a harvest of applause. Bazil somewhat acridly remarked on a later occasion that being President was an asset, even in the field of literature.

---

(1) President Trujillo was a close friend of Bazil whom he aided with financial means. He appointed him to important diplomatic positions in Europe and Latin American capitals, and his generous assistance was ever forthcoming. After the poet's death he had impressive ceremonies held in his memory in the Cathedral in San Cristóbal and gave the illustrous poet's name to the Osvaldo Bazil Institute of Poetry which Trujillo created in that historic city. Bazil, in turn, was a sincere admirer and supporter of President Trujillo, as well as a staunch and loyal friend. He could not have been otherwise. He was a true friend, frank and consistent, selfless. Noble and sincere as a poet, he was tender, romantic, and a dreamer.

CHAPTER VI

ATTRIBUTES OF CHARACTER

A human being's personality results from various ethnic, genealogical, environmental, and educational factors that exert a decisive influence by determining and molding his character. To understand Trujillo today one must be acquainted with the Trujillo of yesteryear.

A study of Trujillo as an adolescent and as a young man is necessary for insight into the meaning of the relentless fight he has waged, his innermost aspirations, the obstacles he had to hurdle, the disappointments and setbacks of all sorts that he suffered and had to overcome before occupying his unique place in the forefront of Dominican life. In his life all has not been sweetness and light. He has had to contend with calumny, treacherous attacks, arrogant hypocrisy, and covert envy. Had Trujillo been of a vengeful bent, these would have been more than sufficient to embitter his spirit, but he is quick to forgive, however strong his initial resentment may be. His sense of dignity is above hate. He does not lose mastery over his emotions. He metes out punishment with stern objectivity as a court of justice would, that is, deliberately and without the heat of personal passion.

He won against those obstacles we had cited, and one must admit that few men have attained in their lifetime so thorough and absolute a success as Generalissimo Trujillo has.

In men tempered as he, obstacles are an incentive, hazards a spur, and disappointements a challenge.

Inspired by an entirely democratic and thoroughly Dominican spirit, Trujillo has acted in defiance of all dissociating social, racial or political differences. Feudal arbiters of society; bloated political leaders; vain, mediocre intellectuals—the whole flock of parasites of yore who fed on the body politic, accustomed to finding among their fellow men a cowardly complicity, were suddenly hurled from their plush positions and forced to put their shouldiers to the wheel and to do their share toward the rebirth of their country planned by Trujillo. This political and social transformation is still being carried out.

Trujillo is a man who never loses sight of his main objective. He knows what he wants and how to attain it. He leaves nothing to chance and all his plans include alternate courses to meet any contingencies that may arise. It is difficult to catch him unawares; it is generally he who takes others unawares. When he was only twenty years old, he said to a friend, "I am going to join the Army and I won't be satisfied until I hold its highest rank". Nor did he stop there, although he was never one to let ambition get the best of him.

When President Vásquez extended his own term of office in 1928, Trujillo already was the most powerful man in the country. Holding in his hands control over the armed forces, he also controlled everything else —peace, war, national stability. Only the purblind would deny this. Still, he never risked a leap that might end in a fall. His self-control, coupled with his passion for outdoing himself, always saved him from any abyss.

Without losing that self-control and precisely because of it, without ever departing from the strictes discipline, he remained calm and aloof and stayed at his post, though suffering at the sight of the mess, the corruption, and the chaotic conditions of an administration that was bent on suicide by not heeding any warning. He resisted the constant urgings of impatient fellow-citizens and any temptation that may have been put in his way to use the overwhelming armed strenght and all-powerful resources at his command. Although audacious by nature, he remained collected, his bravery being of a deliberate and cool type rather than the impulsive and spectacular. Smothering his bitter feelings he waited. Biding his time, which he knew full well wold come, he watched events play into his hands. And his hour struck, at exactly the right moment. For such were his personal traits; such, too, were the unforseen circumstances in wich the country found itself enmeshed, with the traditional political parties totally discredited while a disillusioned people had given up all hope. No juncture in the past wold have lent itself so perfectly for Trujillo's rescue of his people. That is what made his advent so completely provindential and timely.

His election as President of the Republic in 1930 was, therefore, the natural and logical outcome of all his prior actions.

Up until that time the Dominican people, throughout their history as an independent nation, had naught but reasons to bewail disconsolately their cruel and undeserved fate.

Of a sudden, like a flash of light breaking through darkness, Trujillo's election opened wide the gates of hope.

His election did not come about as result of political machinations of the sort that almost invariably are devoid of any lofty ideals and are linked to a spoils system; nor was it the result of the still baser underhanded scheming of selfish interests forever barricaded behind privileges and monopolies that counter true national prosperity; nor was it an outcropping of overt or covert foreign inflences whose ultimate designs an alert patriotims would reject as boding ill for the country. He was the choice of unerring popular feeling —that prescient intuition whereby in times of grave crisis, the people change the course of destiny by choosing a savior.

Such a man could not fail to achievs results. Though luck was not always on his side, he has hurdled all obstacles. Only those persons who have been privileged to be near him in trying and desperate moments; those who have seen him struggle hour after hour, day after day, incessantly, untiringly, for the solution of seemingly insurmountable difficulties, rising to any occasion when others would become discouraged, only those persons can realize fully the toll in sacrifices, sleepless nights, mental torture, and arduous planning for that colossal achievement later referred to simply, as though it were without importance, in the words, "The budget has been balanced".

Those persons who have been near him know of the exhausting daily grind involved in holding in one's hands, alone, the tangled skein of politics as tortuous, complicated and disappointing as Dominican politics have been; in having to see, listen to and talk with so many different men, each with his own burden of sorrow, needs, hopes or, sometimes, even treachery; in having to bear patiently with so much truth and so much falsehood; and, when in the midst of the most abstruse problems of state, having to rush off somewhere to cope, at grave personal danger, with subversion whenever it has assailed the nation. Only those persons near him are aware of the toll exacted in moral suffering, unshared disappointments, and personal anguish by that colossal task which we have referred to and which often is described simply, as though it were without importance, in the words, "The country enjoys peace."

An outstanding factor in Trujillo's character and that which has contributed the most to his natural proclivity for self-control and to the ordering of his habits is his strictly military training which began in early youth. Military discipline imbued him with ideas of moderation at that stage of life when youthful imagination, drawn to the easy pleasures of wine, women and song, readily succumbs to all sorts of temptation.

He is devoid of hypocritical austerity, social puritanism, and those pharisaical attitudes that oftentimes are used to conceal moral failings; but his rather frank and cordial jovialty never reaches extremes. He has enjoyed the pleasures of the world, but exercising withal a proper control. The fifteen years of barracks life were devoted to setting an example for his subordinates.

Patriotism and a thirst for glory, valor and intelligence —these form the keynotes of his strong personality. They are as four granite columns that have supported his astonishing success in the field of government.

His sense of human values and the lessons he has learned from that peerless teacher, life, which have left their imprint in his very soul, have made Generalissimo Trujillo an understanding man.

One cannot speak of his outstanding qualities without underscoring, as a wellspring of his noble sentiments, the gallant, humane, sincere and abiding generosity of his spirit. His unheralded philanthropic endeavors, the encouragement and aid he has tendered in a spontaneous manner and without ostentation, are constant and without number. There isn't a single hamlet in the Republic, no matter how small and humble, where there are not hearts that are grateful for his timely and unmeasured munificence. His selfless giving has been without ulterior motives or artifice, with no political showmanship, springing solely from his natural inclination toward chivalrous and generous acts. All those who have worked close to him know that when Generalissimo Trujillo has extended his friendly and prodigal hand it has been without any hope of recompense and with that intimate satisfaction that altruists derive from the knowledge that they have contributed to alleviating the suffering of their fellow men, and to their welfare. Such is his nature. He is a sentimentalist. Just as treachery will arouse in him fiery ire, sincere anguish or an undeserved misfortune moves him immediately to pity. He is not wont to hearing with indifference the plaints of others, nor will his eyes view disdainfully a hand stretched out imploringly. Whenever he is made aware of the presence of grief his heart becomes filled with tender mercy.

CHAPTER VII

CHARACTER KEYNOTE

There is in every individual some predominant moral trait, be it good or evil, to which all other notes of his character are subordinate. All his passions, all his affections, and all other inclinations, be they apposite or related, become of secondary importance. For example, in a hardened miser, whatever other faults, virtues, vices, desires or passions he may have are overridden by that dominant, basic sentiment. If he is coward, his very avarice inspires him with courage; if he is lecherous, his avarice may make him chaste; if his mind is obtuse, his insatiable greed may make him shrewd, and despite his moral perverseness and his innate inclination toward vice, the fear of spending money may make him, socially, a paragon of virtue.

In Trujillo's case, his glowing success is owed to the happy blending of the fundamental principles that forged his character. His high patriotism, his thirst for glory and his desire to outdo himself, particularly, clearly set him apart as a superior man.

Unlike the king of France who said, "Aprés moi le déluge", and the Dominican president who, reminded of his responsibility before history, boasted cynically, "I won't be around to read my history", Trujillo, in all his actions, is ever mindful of posterity's judgment. This is only natural in one who loves glory and undying fame as much as he does.

Without that ambition for immortality, without that striving to outdo himself, there would be no understanding Trujillo. Moreover, lacking those two qualities and were he devoid of his relevant patriotism, he would not occupy in history the place he has already won. As President he has been quite the opposite of other chief executives, and what no other President before him ever was—a thoroughgoing Dominican who in his exalted, militant and proud patriotism seeks to obtain his highest reward in seeing his country's flag on high and in earning the trust and love of his fellow countrymen. No one has succeeded as much as he in arousing the dormant sense of their own dignity among the Dominican people; no one was ever able as he to inspire among them—after they had lost all hope—faith in themselves and in the imperishable greatness of their destiny.

The three men who prior to 1930 stand out most in the political history of the Dominican Republic because of both the duration of their respective tenures of office and the undeniable influence they exerted upon the life of the nation are unquestionably Santana, Báez and Heureaux. Each of them filled an era. Those before and after them were not of sufficient stature to dominate. Those three, however, undoubtedly possessed extraordinary qualifications. Yet, neither Santana's magnificent and legendary bravery, Báez' sharp intelligence, nor Heureaux's wily foxiness and unparallelled psychological insight have been of themselves sufficient to wipe out the memory of their terrible downfall and the regrettable blots on their records. Santana, whose victorious sword achieved our independence from the Haitian invaders, lost faith in the permanence of the Republic and arranged annexation by Spain; Báez, a true popular leader, and one of the most able men of his day, leased Samaná Bay and sought a United States protectorate; Heureaux brought about the country's ruin through onerous debts and ceded to Haiti, the Dominican Republic's traditional enemy, a strip of the nation's territory, for money. Lacking in ideals, they thought of nothing but power, the selfish enjoyment of power. Never was the nation itself the uppermost thing in their thought. They lacked faith in their country's destiny because all of them were without that which Trujillo has in such abundant measure —patriotism. We Dominicans now are certain that after Trujillo's example at the helm, no one who may come after him, no matter how evil and cynical such a person may be, will dare to traffic with so sacred a trust as the nation itself. Trujillo has laid down the norms. In the pages of history his name shall ever be as a standard for future generations to follow in honor and dignity.

There were some who, in the early stages of his political life, regarded Trujillo as an upstart. That is, an upstart because he was not a graduate of the University; a parvenu because he had not engaged in politics nor in any uprising. This unfortunate misconception has subsequently been regretted by those who in the beginning sought to block his path; their regret, however, was quite unnecessary, inasmuch as a long time ago he already forgave everything — the gratuitous condemnation, the contempt of the vain, the calumnies of the envious, and the conspiracies of assassins, thereby displaying a conciliatory and tolerant spirit that proved to the world that Trujillo did not want to be the President of a clique or a party, as all his predecessors were, but, rather, that he wanted to be and is the leader of all the Dominican people.

Unthinking persons of frivolous mind and accustomed to viewing things superficially as a rule attribute to Generalissimo Trujillo's actions an intent or purpose that is nearly always contrary to the truth. In their hasty judgment they do not stop to reflect that at times one must dig deep, search far back in the past or probe very thoroughly in order to find the key to the enigma of Trujillo. Being themselves incapable of sacrifice for any moral, noble and worthy cause, they do not conceive, they cannot conceive that there should be anyone who might devote his whole life obdurately and wholeheartedly to achieving a patriotic ideal.

To a large extent, such a lack of understanding is due to the absence of mental suppleness among the majority of Dominican politicians. Clinging to reactionary historical opinions, and stultified by a prevalent cowardice, either wittingly or unwittingly they have failed to realize that, with the former molds shattered and the systems of the past discarded, President Trujillo's political ideology has been and is substantially, and at times in form also, openly revolutionary. Revolutionary in methods and, above all, in its goals.

A peaceful revolution, without bloodshed or strife, still it implies a complete and transcendental transformation of administrative procedures and of the idea of what constitutes good government for the people of the Dominican Republic.

That failure to grasp this truth and to understand his objectives and ideals has been an added incentive rather than an obstacle for the Generalissimo. Isolation has been for him a source of strength—strength to concentrate upon his ideas, strength to gather energy, and strength for arduous mental training. That which is a source of discouragement to others, in his case serves to bring to the fore hidden resources. His youthful enthusiasm rekindled fires that his tired forerunners had permitted to die through neglect.

In the light of that general incomprehension among the so-called politicians one can readily understand why they found the Generalissimo so enigmatic and difficult a figure. He has so many facets! As time goes on new and hitherto unsuspected spiritual qualities are found in him; an entirely unknown aspect, a new modality, an unexpected and astonishing reaction is revealed.

His decisions are almost invariably surprising, for Trujillo is unpredictable indeed. Still, even the least of the Generalissimo's deeds has some sound basis and serves an important purpose.

In the supposition that he was motivated by kindred passions, inclinations and purposes as the politicians of yore, it was thought that he could be measured with the same yardstick. This explains the regrettable error of those who at first sought to block his way. He ignored them, and turning to the people —the real people, the long-suffering and hard-working people— he addressed to them these prophetic words, "You can follow me without fear". And the people put their trust in him and followed him to a man.

As was said before, unawareness of Trujillo's mind explains why at the outset he was not judged fairly and objectively, and also why he was treated as an upstart, when he is the very antithesis of those politicians who achieve power through a coup or by some whim of fortune; he is likewise the antithesis of the professional leader who is raised above the common herd by either partisan interest or passion. Everything in him is the result of cool, calculated study. He does not await opportunity's knock, but creates and controls opportunity itself.

Hence the fact that Trujillo is the author of his own success, a success unlike the sporadic one that luck may bring. It is, rather, the success that stems from a man's intrinsic qualities. It is of a lasting nature, the product of efficiency, system, character, and uncommon organizing ability. His military career is a living example of all this, marked as it was by steady, upward progress without skipping grades from Lieutenant to Captain, to Major, to Colonel, to General, and, finally, to Generalissimo. Step by step, grade by grade, ever onward, without a single halt or hiatus. He is undoubtedly a clear example of the fact that success does not depend upon luck, and that it requires extraordinary physical and mental qualities, dynamic impulse, prior preparation, discipline, and persevering effort. It demands an unswerving pursuit of a goal and an obstinate dedication without either flinching from the greatest exertions nor overlooking the minutest detail; it calls for physical as well as moral courage which bows before no setback or obstacle. Success is not the fruit of chance. It is the product of will power and character. What has been described as the good fortune or the "star" of great men consists, in the main, of their adaptation and molding of the milieu wherein they are to put into play their innate qualities in order to attain their essential objectives, and in their wisdom and resolve to avail themselves of favorable circumstances. The resources and the ability of all true geniuses are inborn, and therefore only for God to give or deny.

CHAPTER VIII

A POLITICAL FIGURE BUT NOT A POLITICIAN

Taking the word in the meaning which we generally give it, Trujillo never was what is known as a politician. His proclivities as an eager youth did not lead him into those channels. In those days, to say that a man was a Dominican politician was tantamount to calling him a revolutionist opposed to law and order. Trujillo has been and is quite the opposite of that. His character and his whole moral structure are cast in the mold of patient, orderly action, with an unhurried, methodical, progressive development, but firm and steady. He takes things by stages.

Life has made him a devotee of discipline. Obedience, punctuality, selfcontrol and a subconscious habit of being always attentive and awake to the voice of conscience are second nature in him. He has a firm conviction that without discipline order is impossible, and that without order peace is impossible. For this reason he is harsh in punishing any breach of discipline, which he feels borders on disloyalty.

It did not take him long to realize that one of the most serious defects among the Dominican people was a lack of discipline, and that only through strict discipline could their unruly and rebellious nature and their individualistic tendencies —so independent of guidance— be corrected or modified. He viewed the rigorous imposition of discipline as a **sine qua non** in order to obtain positive and effective results for his country.

So that his lofty aims and long range plans might be brought to the people without any adulterations, President Trujillo had to have cooperation from a political body capable of informing the people. None of the parties that existed when he came into power was capable of fulfilling that need. Unencumbered by any prior political commitments ,he had complete freedom to decide what would best further his aims. He decided to establish a new party, but it was to be a party capable of supporting, through intimate contact with the people of the country, the program designed by him for their redemption. The **Partido Dominicano** (Dominican Party) was the product of that decision.

All the other parties were based upon the personal type of politics devoid of ideals prevalent in the country prior to 1930. Rightly did President Trujillo state in the most important speech of all his political career, "The Dominican Party is an all-out effort to form an organization capable of overcoming the system of personal, factious politics of groups that have no program to offer." (1)

---

(1) This notable speech was delivered by President Trujillo at the opening of the XIII Pan American Sanitary Conference and aroused great interest in the Dominican Republic and abroad. His regime's irreconcilable enemies who heard or read this speech must have felt uncomfortable indeed.

With characteristic accuracy, in his **Visión de un Pueblo,** Gerardo Gallegos says of President Trujillo's famous speech the following: "As a veteran journalist in the Western Hemisphere, I have heard protocolary statements by oustanding statesmen in various capitals. However, I do not recall ever having heard another speech that rang as true as this

From the outset, the Dominican Party has aimed toward national unity. It has also had an uplifting mission which President Trujillo has defined thus, "Without a working body, without a live and active organization, without a flexible, disciplined and responsible force that would identify itself with the reconstruction sought by the Government, the achievement of those aims, which of course could not be attained in a single day by one man alone, would have been impossible. When I conceived the idea of creating a Dominican Party I was not thinking of merely another political party but of establishing a Dominican social sub-structure that would be capable of accomplishing by itself the vital program for a general transformation that would determine the life of the country as a whole. By an imperative mandate stemming from our social conditions, the Party has proved a civilizing force".

Because the Dominican Party has been uncontested in several general elections it has been compared and invidiously likened to the totalitarian parties created by Communism and Fascism under their single-party systems. This is an utter fallacy. President Trujillo himself has this to say, "On several occasions we have been accused of operating the Dominican Party as though we had a single-party system, wherein there would be no opportunity

one, any so fraught with deep, bitter and dramatic truths, and, at the same time, so full of sincerity in its conviction of victory and progress achieved after a century and a quarter of a nation's history, as the Dominican President Rafael Leonidas Trujillo's resounding words before the delegates of twenty-three nations present at the Conference who were gathered in the hall of the Caryatides, and which were broadcast throughout the Dominican Republic and the Americas."

whatsoever for opposition. This accusation is unfounded, because the Party's original membership comprised the former members of the old parties that fell apart through weariness and a lack of faith in their own objectives. I wish to point out that my administration has included men from all the political groups existing prior to 1930 as well as some individuals who never had anything to do with those groups. It is obvious that we have brought about a new awareness of the meaning of partisanship that will not permit a return to the discarded system of amorphous and motley factions whose activities in years gone by brought many evils to the Republic and gave rise to the breakdown of Dominican democracy. Independently of the influence exerted by the government Party, public opinion has progressed smoothly toward a definite awareness of labor problems and toward the embodiment of women's rights within the country's political and civil framework. Both these achievements are, necessarily, the result of contemporary political trends paralleling governmental action but quite independent of the latter".

Years after the Dominican Party was in active operation, President Trujillo, ever aware of the importance of progress, realized that the Party's program suffered from a certain rigidity and a marked conservative tendency. He immediately initiated a thorough reform of its Charter, imparting thereto an orientation more in keeping with present-day conditions and furthering the reasonable and just aspirations of labor for social justice as well as the deep-rooted liberal hopes of the masses. That suppleness of the Dominican Party accounts for its greatest triumphs.

The new Statement of Principles of the Dominican Party sets forth, among others, the following excellent postulates: "The Dominican Party maintains as an integral part of its program the postulates of the Right to Work and of Social Justice". "It is a basic tenet of the Dominican Party that all men are born equal and should enjoy equal opportunity, and it therefore repudiates any discrimination based on class, race or creed". "The civil and political equality of the sexes is a tenet of the Dominican Party." "Considering that freedom and democracy are essential elements of all community life, the Dominican Party always has advocated and will continue to strive to the end that the activities of the Dominican people in all their manifestations may develop in an atmosphere of absolute freedom and in keeping with democratic principles."

The Dominican Party is unlike the political parties which divided among themselves the country prior to 1930 and were, rather than institutions built around principles, mere factions built around selfish interests, and it also differs widely from the important historical parties that in the most powerful nations of the world serve as political channels during short periods of time just before elections and that are the rallying points for intense struggles between rival candidates. The Dominican Party, on the contrary, is an institution with permanent character, with buildings of its own, many of them real palaces, with a year-round, full-time staff and unending work; it is primarily an institution devoted to the furthering of cultural and civic progress and material and moral cooperation toward the high ideas championed by its distinguished founder.

Its various headquarters, even in the most remote corners of the Republic, are real centers of culture and art, where lectures, concerts and other scientific and literary events are held and contribute in a decided manner to raising the moral and intellectual level of the people.

Another important activity of the Dominican Party is the publication of books by both national and foreign authors that will contribute in one way or another to the enhancement of the Republic's good name and the dissemination of culture among its people. The Party is, moreover, an unfailing promoter of public welfare. The first modern social welfare activities in the Republic (free distribution of milk, bread and clothing; low-cost housing developments, and free medical assistance) were carried out and financed by the Dominican Party.

For all these reasons those foreigners who, upon visiting our country, learn of the Party's real activities, are unbounded in their praise and admiration. Although without legal or official standing as such, the Dominican Party has become a new institution of the State.

There is no doubt but that President Trujillo has achieved the greatest success in creating the Dominican Party. It can be said that its membership rolls constitute a true electoral census of the voting male and female population of the country.

CHAPTER IX

TRUJILLO IN POLITICS

Trujillo is no dilettante in politics nor does he take it lightly. Aware of the grave responsibility upon his shoulders and of the overwhelming magnitude of the task of national reconstruction he has accomplished, he does not delegate his leadership. He is forever on the alert, watchful and cautious. In his mind's eye he follows closely the actions of all those in the public limelight, be they friends or otherwise; he studies what they do and looks for details that are generally neglected by others. He forms his plans by himself alone, for which reason those persons surrounding him wield scant or no influence at all upon his decisions. Those individuals whom the public may believe to be his chosen friends or confidants either because they are very close to him or because they hold high office, at times may be as fully ignorant of his secrets of state as the man in the street, save in what may pertain to matters that have been entrusted to them directly. He is an indefatigable worker. In his wonderful and thoroughly documented book, "I Was Trujillo's Secretary" **(Yo fuí Secretario de Trujillo)**, Dr. José Almoina rightly states that, "Working with Trujillo leaves time for neither rest nor relaxation; he is physically and intellectually made of steel and his speed at work allows neither pause nor delay. He demands an extraordinary capacity for work that few can stand." (1) Trujillo does not have any advisors. Reserving his thoughts to himself, he is sphinx-like. Several of his subordinates may be engaged at a given moment in carrying out one of his plans, but each is cognizant only of that part which concerns him and is ignorant of the rest. No one, not even his seemingly closest friend, has ever been able to say that he knows as much as Trujillo about his political thought and activities. Trujillo never plays into the hands of either friends or enemies. He is altogether too powerful for cliques to succeed with him. His mistrust, his innate suspiciousness will ever keep him free from that political error that has worked the downfall of so many statesmen in the Americas —that the President himself be the one to arm the hand or build up the prestige of someone who will succeed him, or that his administration's formidable strength to face its enemies should turn out to be, in the long run, propitious for ambitious men to prosper in his shadow. Keeping himself ready for any political or military emergency, his astuteness and unfailing instinct have always stood him well. His equanimity in the face of uncertainty is paralleled only by his quickness of action once his suspicions are confirmed.

Indeed, he does take politics seriously and expects everyone else to do likewise. There have been no exceptions to this rule.

---

(1) A very true statement. I can bear witness to it because I too was Trujillo's Secretary.

This, in general outline, is the man. Spurred on by the very greatness of the task he has undertaken —a mission that must not be blighted by selfishness nor destroyed by error— Generalissimo Trujillo pursues undauntedly, with the clear vision of a prophet, the arduous and heartbreaking path of glory. He draws inspiration from his patriotism alone, a patriotism that is ever greater in keeping with the new horizons that open before it with each new achievement.

Trujillo, like every miracle-worker, is exhilarated by the wine of his prodigious accomplisments and draws strength from them for further conquests. He is never satisfied. He is ever outdoing himself. A job accomplished no longer holds any interest for him. His eyes are ever fixed upon the future, upon what remains to be done for his country's prosperity, its greatness and its glory.

Bear in mind that your home holds your happiness and your honor.

Rafael L. Trujillo

CHAPTER X

FAMILY LIFE OF THE PRESIDENT

President Trujillo maintains residence in various parts of the country for the purpose of staying there during his various trips, but his official residence or home is located in the suburbs of Ciudad Trujillo, on Kilometer 3 of Carretera Sánchez, at the end of Independencia Avenue. This beautiful estate, named "Estancia Ramfis" for his eldest son, Captain Rafael L. Trujillo Martínez, has every comfort for a family's health, recreation and well-being —reception, study, entertainment and sewing rooms, lounges; a library, and bars; a dentist's office, a swimming pool, a gym, a motion picture theatre, a barber shop and beauty parlors; luxurious dining halls, etc. It also has suitable quarters for the military guard. That is his refuge and haven of rest and recreation away from the taxing duties of each day. There the President lives with his family. It is his home.

There, in the company of his beautiful and brilliant wife, Doña María de los Angeles Martínez de Trujillo, and their three children, Captain Rafael L. Trujillo Martínez, Angelita del Corazón de Jesús and little Radhamés, amid a virtuous home environment warmed by mutual love, the statesman finds rest from his patriotic cares and garners what is to him the richest reward this earth can hold—love from his family.

A model husband, and an affectionate brother and kind kinsman toward all his relatives, he is above all a loving father. His concern for the welfare of his children, including the care of their health and attention to their studies as well as their play, is always evident.

His unbounded love for his son Ramfis brought suffering to President Trujillo's heart when the former was stricken, at the age of seven, with a serious illness that endangered his life. There was no question of any restraint in his demonstrations of affection for the boy, and there seemed to be no ameliorating the deep worry he felt.

The President, who has always been an untiring worker of a truly uncommon fiber, seemed at times beaten and exhausted, worn by the long vigil silently borne in order to inspire courage among others. Finally, the seemingly endless hours of anguish and prayerful hope were rewarded with the child's complete recovery.

The first Lady of the Land shares, understandingly and loyally, the President's worries and his joys. Endowed with a brilliant cultivated mind, Doña María lends great dignity to her difficult role as First Lady. Her exquisite tact, and her exemplary dignified manner are ever evident. Her share in the President's public life is not of the publicity-seeking kind indulged in by other women of high station who have taken a hand in politics. Her lofty idea of her vocation as mistress of her own home and of her station in society and in the world at large is reflected in her literary articles in her popular and justly praised book entitled

Meditaciones Morales ("Moral Meditations"), and in her successful play **Falsa Amistad** ("False Friendship") ,in which works she reveals, with a skilfull style, her deep religious convictions, her enormous culture which is molded along so-called old-fashioned lines, her modern outlook, and her home training which awakened in her soul an abiding Christian piety and lends an aristocratic note as well as diamond-hard firmness to her friendship. She is not a believer in that type of feminine activity that oftentimes launches women upon political careers, but rather in the quiet, persuasive influence that a mother can exert by developing love of country in the home and shaping the character and the future of her offspring, and she believes in the good example that a woman of high station in society should set in matters such as deportment and which will be reflected in service of country and of God.

The daughter of parents who came many years ago directly from the mother country, Spain, and who achieved as members of our best society the formation of a highly respected household, Doña María possesses a type of beauty that is a credit to her pure Spanish blood. Her large, dark but wide-awake eyes, finely drawn mouth, her strong profile, her beautiful black hair that is becomingly covered by a lace shawl over a high comb when she goes to church, her small and soft hands with which she elegantly punctuates her speech in Latin fashion but without exaggeration, all these make her a prototype of Spanish beauty.

But Doña María's moral qualities are even more deserving of praise than her physical beauty. Her inclination to all that is good makes her lend at every opportunity her enthusiastic support for any welfare undertaking that may have as its purpose the alleviation of human suffering, and to efforts for educational and moral uplifting that may bring about a greater amount of learning among the rising generation to whom are entrusted all our hopes for the future.

The guidance that she has given through her literary and philosophical works to male as well as female Dominican youth cannot be understood in all its worth at the present time, since it is something planned with the future in mind. She has planted seeds that will require years before coming into full fruition, but the loving doctrine she preaches to the young people must certainly bear results when they have become adult citizens.

Doña María's social and literary work has been acclaimed both within and without the country's frontiers and has brought her many tributes from various institutions and governments. She has had bestowed upon her the Grand Cross of the French Legion of Honor, the Grand Cross of the Order of Duarte, that of the Order of Trujillo, as well as that of the Dominican Red Cross, the Grand Cross of the Cuban Red Cross, and other precious awards. The Civic Social League of Puerto Rican Women proclaimed her, by unanimous vote, "The most outstanding woman of the Caribbean area" because of her edifying accomplishments in behalf of women and children. She was proclaimed an honorary citizen of the city of Santiago de los Caballeros, second largest population center in the Dominican Republic, and several institutions, schools, parks and streets in different parts of the country have been named in her honor.

The first-born of the distinguished Trujillo couple, Captain Rafael L. Trujillo Martínez, is now twenty-one years old and is a fourth-year student in the School of Law of the University of Santo Domingo. He attained his present military rank after having completed studies at the Training Center of the Dominican Army, in which he enrolled as a Cadet. He took courses for the consular and diplomatic service in the special school that the Dominican Foreign Office operated for a period of several years.

Ramfis, as he is affectionately nicknamed by members of his family and intimate friends, is a bright young man, well-mannered, unassuming, cultured, and affable though of serious bent. He is an able sportsman, a good soldier and very popular in social circles. His father is proud of his eldest son as well he may. As the saying goes, "Like father, like son", and scarce else need be added. Born in the lap of luxury and wealth, nonetheless he was reared in an atmosphere of reverence for work and discipline. Hence the serious mind we have mentioned that lies behind his youthfully buoyant character. Studious, obedient, always observing the best manners, friendly and courteous, an interesting conversationalist, he has won the hearts of people everywhere. Ramfis is a source of pride not only to his parents but to his countrymen, who have great hopes for his future in a not too distant day.

The other children of the Trujillo-Martínez couple are still very young. Both are in full formative years. Angelita, a picture of adolescent grace, is a pupil in the Colegio "Santo Domingo", and the youngest, Leonidas Rhadamés, a bright and restless lad, in the Colegio De La Salle. At home, the twigs are bent in the direction of virtue and good.

CHAPTER XI

FRONT AND CENTER

Underground lodes containning great mineral wealth that are discovered from time to time in various places of the earth are the result of an evolution which has taken centuries upon centuries, of the accumulation over thousands of years of layers, one upon the other. They are rarely found, and this explains their value. In mankind's evolutionary process one generation follows another as so many strata, and a great many years come and go, sometimes even centuries, before there comes to the fore on life's stage, as by the hand of Providence, a truly uncommon man, a superior being who is able to change the fate of his country. Just as a fine bloom is brought into being by roots whose chain of life extends far into the past and responds to the occult forces of nature, so it is with that rare man who is to make a real mark upon history.

The man we speak of is by no means an improvisation. His gigantic stature projects itself into the distant future, after many generations have passed, molding the thoughts, the habits and the very lives of those who will come after him.

When no one gives much thought any longer to his spectacular military victories, Napoleón's Civil Code still directs the course of life in France, and his memory as a military leader is eclipsed by that of his statesmanship in dictating that code. When, after more than a century, the wake his troops left behind becomes blurred, still his revolutionary thoughts and the political consequences of his actions are to be felt. He was truly an uncommon man who left a definite work mark upon history for all time.

Our contemporary records afford few names that have won immortality for themselves and brought undying fame to their countries. Germany's Bismarck; Russia's Lenin; the Ottoman Kemal Ataturk, who had in himself the political sagacity of Bismarck and the revolutionary spirit of Lenin. That is what made Kemal one of the greatest Europeans in contemporary history.

Blanco Villalta, the Argentine biographer of Kemal, says of him, "When the Turkish people were bowing before destiny, there appeared the man who would change the course of history in the East: Kemal Ataturk. To this man Turkey owes the salvation of its land, the transformation of its decadent empire into a flourishing republic, and the redemption of its people. This man, a master in democracy, is one of the great founders, fully of the stature of those whose names stand out in history and whose memory the peoples venerate".

"Circumstances, the fanaticism and backwardness to which his people adhered, forced him to impose a strong-arm régime without which it would have been impossible to accomplish the country's change and reaction would have overcome reform, throwing back all progress. Otherwise the transformation from fierce Ottoman autocracy to the most advanced democracy would not have been feasible. A period of education and acclimatization was required. Kemal, the master, unceasingly prepared the people of his country so they could understand those ideals".

"Kemal is probably the most interesting ruler and of the post-war leaders probably the purest, at heart, if one takes into account the spiritual benefits his people derived."

Years after his death, his finest masterwork, the salvation of his country, becomes greater and stronger with each passing day. Kemal's wielding of power in Turkey is stamped with the seal of those things that are definite and everlasting.

No two men are identical; history's heroes may be similar in their achievements but not in their persons. However, if one wants to compare President Trujillo with some other great reformer of a nation who stands out in modern times because of his revolutionary and constructive accomplisments, we believe that none has as many traits in common with our own Generalissimo as Kemal Ataturk, the genius who built the new Turkey, save for accidents of time and their respective milieus.

Both were professional soldiers and both were imbued with an abiding sense of patriotism that inspired their untiring creative efforts. Both had to overcome the same odds —selfishness, envy, calumny, and deep misunderstanding. Both had to contend with a lack of preparation among their people in a moral, cultural and material sense, with ingrained rebelliousness, and with a lack of capable helpers. But rising in the face of all obstacles, avidly pursuing glory, they achieved in a mere handful of years what countless generations had been unable to attain over centuries. Thus each became in his country the greatest leader it ever had.

Upon undertaking a total reconstruction of their nations through the introduction of thorough-going and truly revolutionary reforms that have aroused a new awareness among the population and inspired new fervor and a fresh feeling of emotion on hearing their respective anthems and seeing their national banners, they had to fight deeply held prejudices dating from far back before their time. A tradition of partisan leadership stood in their way. Even more than their avowed enemies, they had to overcome ingratitude in their own followers, decadent inertia, mutual dislikes among contending parties, shiftlessness and indifference.

Both began their great missions from the same position —leadership of the army. Their first step was to modernize their respective armies, making them efficient toward three ends: first, so those armed forces would be able to maintain peace; second, to ensure the development of a new order in the administrative field, and third, so that those armies might become effective forces supporting public authority so that there could be brought about a social justice that, by freeing the industrial and agricultural workers, would steer them into the wide avenues of happiness and progress.

They both seem alike in their unflinching attitude in the face of foreign intrusion in state matters, until they finally were able — through mental firmness, individual stamina and an irreproachable conduct in the administration of office— to destroy the former status of either country as a vassal and to win international respect for their lands. For political oppression and economic oppression are different forms of one and the same evil—national slavery. As the Argentinian Perón has stated in an immortal phrase, "Comparing one slavery with another, one cannot say which is the worse form."

That staunch attitude, that unrelenting fight to obtain an untrammeled national sovereignty rescued from foreign usurpers is precisely what makes them, for all men to see, true liberators of their peoples.

Neither of the two may be regarded as a professional politician. Still, they turned out to be expert and far-seeing statesmen. Few men have equalled them in the skill with which they brought just the right amount of pressure to bear to gain the objects they pursued.

Both military leaders scaled the highest political power with the support of their countrymen and both —despite being professional soldiers and as such ready, because of their military training, to reach drastic decisions for the maintenance of order and the preservation of peace— instead of restricting individual liberty and abetting ignorance, prepared the people, through well ordered discipline and education, for an increasing measure of real democracy, thus avoiding that the practices of freedom should, as has been the case in certain Western Hemisphere lands, degenerate into license. Above all else, these two builders of nations, Kemal and Trujillo, are united in history by the basic concept and the kindred political creeds which, though expressed in varying forms, they have shared in common, in the sense that any transcendental social reform must, if it is to be of a lasting nature and if it is to go down in history, be supported by that powerful material force which the army comprises together with that immanent moral force which is justice.

PART THREE

THE STATESMAN

CHAPTER XII

THE DOMINICAN REPUBLIC'S CONSTITUTION

Every country's political ideology and psychology are expressed in its Constitution. The principles that are embodied therein lend color to its political banner, for it is through them that its true system of government may be known. Just as reactionary leaders who are systematically opposed to all liberal reforms seek to maintain through the very phrasing of their constitutions a legal foothold for their despotic inclinations, in a democratic atmosphere where there exists an advanced culture and a spirit for civic progress an era's liberal and equalitarian trend is reflected in the principles upon which the nation's charter is based.

Simply because a government is strong and energetic in applying the law —and at times vigorous, caustic and exemplifying action has brought beneficial results— when it comes to punishing or forestalling attacks against the public peace or to imposing responsibility and a spirit of organization and honesty in the administration, it does not necessarily follow that it is a dictatorship. Conversely, because the man who heads an absolute government happens to be weak, timid or vacillating it does not follow that his lack of force necessarily determines the general ideology behind his government. What really matters is the nature of those institutions which guide it and are set forth in the Constitution. If the nation's charter regards human beings as mere tools of the State, as mere machines to work and produce without the right to think for themselves and to seek freely their own happiness; if the government is not based upon the consent of the governed as is the essence of the republican system, if legislative representation is not based upon majority rule and minorities are without representation, the constitution is not a democratic one and we have a totaliatarian or absolute régime.

In several of the countries that have subscribed the Charter of the United Nations constitutional reforms have been essential not only to solve questions of a purely technical or legal character or of adaptation, but also, in certain cases, to buttress a wider and more human application of democratic institutions.

Despite the fact that virtually all the political constitutions of the American Republics are inspired by the Declaration of the Rights of Man and by the Constitution of the United States, guaranteeing man's civil rights, religious freedom, freedom of education, freedom of speech, and freedom of assembly, there still remain some that do not yet guarantee woman's right to citizenship, the civil rights of foreigners, the protection and representation of minorities, and that do not allow the establishment of progressive measures for improving the lot of the working classes, all of which are essential for the fulfillment of any program of forthright human redemption.

Thanks to Trujillo, the Dominican Republic may pride itself in possessing one of the most liberal and democratic constitutions in the world, after the wide reforms effected in 1942, which follow closely the inspiration and personal leadership Generalissimo Trujillo brought to bear as supreme head of the Dominican Party at a time when he was not holding public office. The 1942 reform of our Constitution is based on the most ample concept of social justice and upon the lofty principles that President Trujillo outlined some years before in a message to the National Congress in which he stated with deep-seated conviction that the Dominican Republic is "neither communist nor fascist, but is and shall always be a pure democracy."

We have no need to import political systems from abroad.

Our present Constitution establishes as an immutable principle that the Dominican Republic's form of government is essentially civil, republican, democratic and representative; it establishes elections by secret, direct and universal ballot with prior registration of those who are to cast their vote; it likewise establishes representation of minorities. Citizenship is enjoyed by full right by all persons of either sex who have reached their eighteenth birthday; the President of the Republic and the members of the Senate and the Chamber of Deputies are chosen by direct popular vote; legislation pertaining to the Social Right to Work is authorized; freedom of worship is established; habeas corpus and all those human rights which today make up our civilization's most precious heritage are likewise consecrated.

President Trujillo feels, as he has expressed in several public statements, that the establishment in our country of novel foreign ideologies, even though it should be for the noble and praiseworthy purpose of improving social conditions for the workers or in order to bring about a fuller development of the nation's wealth, is entirely contrary to our way. Hence his persistent, uncompromising opposition to communism, and this is why he was the first head of an American nation to warn of and denounce its dangers as well to uncover its infiltration among our people and to stamp it out drastically. The practical aims of an enligtened socialism can be and have been achieved in ample measure without changing our democratic form of government, which is that generally obtaining throughout Latin America and the form chosen by the express will of majorities in our country from the earliest days of our independence. In fact, it is the only one that, despite the long and tedious process of adaptation and acclimatization that each change of administration has implied, has succeeded in casting deep roots in our soil.

The rigidity that hampered our Constitution prior to the 1942 reform was frequently invoked by reactionary and ill-intentioned elements in our midst in order to impede the adoption in our country of measures furthering social progress and economic government —such as those establishing the Sabbath rest, minimum wages and maximum hours for the working population— by holding that they were unconstitutional. Moreover, with his enlightened foresight that has made him an unparallelled leader, President Trujillo definitely solved that basic difficulty by sponsoring the reform of our obsolete and unyielding former Constitution even before such action should become essential in view of latter day developments. Through that reform, our Constitution establishes as the law of the land the most progressive steps dictated by our civilization, rendering possible, for the first time ,the adoption of humanitarian and liberal measures whose object it is to abolish the enslavement of men by other men and to bring about the dethronement of those monopolies that impede economic progress, while seeking, at the same time, a higher standard of living for the working population, with a concomitant recognition of the rights of labor and the establishment of the principles of social justice that are so essential for human progress and perhaps even dearer than the right to liberty itself.

The scope of the social security and other protective measures given to our land by President Trujillo is such and the liberal and democratic legislation, in keeping with our Constitution, born of his own initiative, is so widespread that their mere enumeration, without mentioning any of his other eminent deeds, would suffice to ensure undying glory for him and to win him a place in any roster of the most progressive leaders in the Americas. Here are some of the most important ones: he initiated laws fixing maximum hours of work and rest on the Sabbath; the distribution of lands, seeds and agricultural tools among needy farmers, accomplished periodically by the Department of Agriculture; minimum wage laws; a law prohibiting payment in scrip; laws establishing retirement rules for military personnel; those ordering the protection of minors, and others creating juvenile courts; anti-illiteracy laws; laws establishing legal and social equality between legitimate offspring; laws rendering marriage easier and lowering or in some cases waiving altogether the fees therefor; compulsory social security for laborers; the establishment of milk stations; school breakfasts; tuberculosis sanatoriums; night normal schools for workers; antivenereal dispensaries; modern housing developments for the working classes and government employees; maternity and post-natal clinics, with free medical services and hospitals even in the most remote sectors of the country.

Specially noteworthy is the Law on Labor Contracts, of June 2, 1944, which reaffirms uncodified regulations that had been enacted on President Trujillo's initiative and also contains provisions that place Dominican labor legislation on a par with the most advanced in matters such as pre-natal and post-natal maternity care, with the payment of salaries and obstetrical attention; health subsidies for workers who may be incapacitated for a given time; indemnity for discharge from employment and outright unemployment; the regulation of arbitration and judicial litigation; laws establishing a Register of Unemployed and an Identification Register for domestic workers, as well as provisions guaranteeing paid vacations for the latter, together with adequate food and other advantages. All this far-reaching, humane and fundamentally Christian legislation is of a socialist pattern in its pursuit of social justice, but completely alien to it is any biased class socialism of the type that at times wields votes for an election as a political weapon, at other times exerts pressure through proletarian strikes as an effective economic weapon, and not infrequently resorts to bombs and firearms in wrathful violence against the existing order.

It must be noted that before President Trujillo came into power, the Dominican Republic had adopted virtually no particular measure for social justice as such. He is the only Chief Executive in the country's history who has officially supported the reasonable expectations of industrial and agricultural workers. At that, he has done so without there having taken place any of the hard fought struggles that give rise to so much hatred and without any demands or threats having been made by labor, without any strikes or armed protests, without socialism, let alone communism, cropping up in our country as a political force. "My best friends are the workingmen", Trujillo stated on one occasion, and his government's deeds bear him out.

In 1946 President Trujillo started a new reform of the Constitution, this time limited to giving the country a sound and wholly national monetary system, and to creating a State banking system. The reform established, among other provisions destined to the same end, that: "The national unit of currency is the gold peso." Under Paragraph I it sets forth that "The only currency legally in circulation and being legal tender shall be those bills issued by an autonomous issuing entity whose capital shall be State property, on condition that the same shall be in their entirety backed by gold reserves and other holdings of real and effective value, in that proportion and under those terms by law ordained and under unlimited guarantee by the State."

President Trujillo has said of these measures, in his Message explaining the same which he sent to the Congress when he requested this reform of the Constitution, "A country's independence and sovereignty do not depend solely upon its political freedom. That freedom becomes merely theoretical if the country does not exercise at the same time financial and economic independence. The Trujillo-Hull Treaty re-established our financial sovereignty. The creation of a Central Bank of the Republic and the issuance of an independent national currency effectively backed by gold and truly representative of the national wealth will constitute the definite establishment and recognition of our monetary and economic sovereignty."

Once the reform was approved, the Central Bank of the Republic was created by Law Number 1529 of October 9, 1947. By virtue of that law the Bank is an autonomous institution, the property of the State, with its own assets and legal capacity. Its establishment came about as a result of detailed studies sponsored by the Chief Executive, with the aid of foreign technical experts, in order to give the country a currency of its own and a banking organization featuring the most up-to-date improvements. Up until the Central Bank's creation and for forty years before that time the United States dollar was exclusively the currency that circulated in the Republic. Prior to that, there circulated the currency of any and all countries, particularly Mexican silver currency. Heureaux issued paper money without any backing and he minted coins that were worth only twenty per cent of their face value at the time of his death. The paper currency had been suddenly demonetized, bringing ruin to countless families.

Among the several functions entrusted to the Central Bank there is that of carrying out all operations converting United States dollars into Dominican gold pesos, a function it has performed with the assistance of the Dominican Republic Reserve Bank and the branch offices of foreign banks located in our country. This process of conversion commenced on October 23, 1947, on which date the first Central Bank bills, of one, five and ten peso denominations, were placed in circulation. The new national currency was enthusiastically taken up by the public, as may be understood from the fact that in the nine days following the start of conversion operations, that is up to October 31, 1947, Dominican Republic peso bills issued totalled $4,884,660, notwithstanding the fact that the United States dollar too was legal tender throughout the entire period of monetary reform which ended on February 1, 1948. By the latter date conversion was practically completed and the second phase of the reform was put into operation. The Dominican gold peso remained henceforth the sole medium of payment under all agreements and contracts excepting specific cases provided in the banking and currency laws.

Subsequently, on April 23, 1948, the International Monetary Fund, an organization for the stabilization of the currency of its member countries, declared international parity for the Dominican gold peso to be .888671 grams of fine gold, in keeping with the standard proposed by the Government of the Dominican Republic. This par value is, in terms of United States dollars, one Dominican gold peso for each United States dollar, and it is based upon the prevailing standard for United States dollars in the Dominican Republic as provided in the Currency Law of October 9, 1947. Consequently, the par value of the Dominican gold peso in terms of the United States dollar is as follows: .888671 grams of fine gold per Dominican peso; 35.00 Dominican pesos per troy ounce of fine gold; one Dominican peso per United States dollar; 100 United States cents per Dominican peso.

Bills issued by the Bank are in denominations of DR$1.00, DR$5.00, DR$10.00, DR$20.00, DR$50.00, DR$100.00, DR$500.00, and DR$1,000.00.

The country's metal currency is coined and placed in circulation by the Central Bank, for the Dominican Republic's amount. Its denominations are 1 cent 5 cents, 25 cents, 50 cents, and DR$1.00.

The issuance of currency is, unquestionably, an attribute of national sovereignty. However, the scandalous frauds perpetrated by Heureaux's administration in coining metal currency and in issuing paper bills brought about such grave economic and financial difficulties for the country and public mistrust reached such a peak that none of the succeeding administrations ever attempted to mint or issue new currency. Ony in an era in which orderly organization and administrative probity obtain, such as in the present Trujillo Era ,has the Republic been able to exercise that right with the general approval and full confidence of the people. This has been one of the great accomplishments of Trujillo's administration, an accomplishment undoubtedly calling for boldness and foresight, and it has been widely praised as such. It is a feat that has gone far in cementing the formidable financial soundness of the Government and implementing the Republic's progress along the road of final economic independence.

CHAPTER XIII

FINANCIAL INDEPENDENCE

If Generalissimo Trujillo were lacking the other qualities he possesses, his rare gifts as an organizer and his idea of discipline alone would have earned him the distinction of being the foremost political figure, the most conscientious, the ablest and the one with the most highly developed sense of responsibility ever to occupy the office of President of the Dominican Republic. His actions as an organizer, reformer, teacher and builder have covered so wide and varied a field that to make an adequate commentary of them would require a whole book.

Every time the comparison is made of the progressive works accomplished in so short a span by President Trujillo with those carried out during more than eighty years of independent national life under earlier administrations, one is moved to ask, "What did those administrations prior to Trujillo's do?" When one is cognizant beforehand of their long record of fraud, mistakes, extravagance and failure, the answer comes fast, as a whiplash by conscience — nothing. They did nothing. If one reads our history from the times of the glorious feats with which our political independence was secured through the pages relating Trujillo's brilliant accomplishments, one's enthusiastic admiration is aroused as it would be upon viewing the play of light against shadows in a painting by Rembrandt.

Truly, the number of projects realized by the Dominican Government in keeping with direct instructions from Generalissimo Trujillo is countless: palaces and other public buildings, schools, asylums, hospitals, the University City, irrigation canals, bridges, roads and highways, boulevards and public parks, arsenals and a naval station, monuments, statues and gardens.

Special mention, however, must be made of two outstanding things. One is the thorough and perfect organization of the Army. The other is the scientific organization of the public Treasury. Lack of organization in the Treasury and in the Army were the two vulnerable points of all the preceding administrations and the direct cause of financial chaos as well as economic and political upheavals. They afforded the pretext, albeit a flimsy and illegal one, for the harsh demands of Yankee imperialism in 1915 —a Military Mission and a Financial Adviser. It led us, step by step ,fatally and inevitably, with one fall after another and with shameful disgrace, to humiliating intervention by the United States with the resultant loss of our national sovereignty.

In order to have some idea of the extent and the seriousness of the situation President Trujillo encountered when he took office in 1930 one must bear in mind that while in 1929 the administration of President Vásquez —without including any income from various loans on which it did not have to make a single payment toward amortization— had at its disposal revenues from general sources amounting to nearly $15,000,000 which were ample for its needs, those selfsame revenues over an equal period, the year 1931, as a result of the world-wide crisis, decreased sharply to $7,350,000, that is, to less than fifty percent. Moreover, while the Vásquez administration had to pay in 1929, in keeping with the provisions of the Convention between the Dominican Republic and the United States, only the accrued interest on the 1922-1926 loans, that is, $1,082,619, Trujillo's administration was obliged to pay from 1931 on, besides the interest charges, large monthly amounts corresponding to the amortization fund, which raised the total annual payments on the foreign debt to the huge sum of $2,890,000, all by reason of commitments undertaken by the preceding administration. That amount was more than one-third of the government's total income, and the sum remaining with which to cover the administration's normal expenses was a mere $4,460,000.

At the time when the nation's affairs were entrusted to Trujillo, the salaries of government employees remained for the most part unpaid. Public education as well as public health and welfare services were ill attended, and demoralization had begun to set in. The public roads that had cost so much to build had to go unrepaired and were in pitiful condition for lack of maintenance. A large number of schools, both urban and rural, had to be closed. Our export products brought ridiculously low prices in foreign markets. The sole financial legacy of the preceding administration was a new floating debt of more than $4,000,000 made for the purpose of meeting unpaid salaries and expenses. The Government's credit reached the nadir point, and President Trujillo oftentimes had to make use of his personal credit or his private capital in order to cover ordinary expenses of the State. The capital city, which is the country's most important population center, was still suffering the results of the terrible hurricane that struck it in 1930; its aqueduct was crumbling, its buildings to a large extent destroyed or else sadly needing repairs, its streets and parks gone, its commercial life tottering with real property values crumbling and real estate owners preyed upon by usurious mortgage lenders. Ruin was on all sides, with complete bankruptcy and paralysis of the whole country's economic life. To put it briefly, the spectre of 1916 once more rose up on the horizon, threatening the Government's very existence and again placing the nation's sovereignty in danger of dishonor and death.

It sickens one's heart to think of the dread experiences the country would have had to undergo were it not for the providential fact that Trujillo was there to straighten out its destiny. What would have been the result of the February 23, 1930 revolution if Trujillo had not been at the head of the Army? How would the Public Treasury have fared in the midst of the existing chaos, with fraud and self-enrichment as accepted administrative norms, in the midst of world-wide crisis, if Trujillo had not been there to bring about order out of such chaos? What would have been the fate of the capital city with 3,000 unburied dead and more than 15,000 injured unattended as a result of the hurricane, if Trujillo had not imposed order by drastic measures? The threat of hunger and thirst; the even worse threat of devastating epidemics; crime and robberies without number that could have been perpetrated in the shadows of the prevailing confusion; the failure of commercial houses and foreclosures. Who else but Trujillo would have been capable of preventing them?

One is filled with horror at the dark prospects that lay before. When balancing the books of Trujillo's accomplishments in office, sight is often lost of the fact that our country's gratitude to him is not only for the countless constructive works he has achieved but also for the sorrow, the tremendous losses and the shame that his being in power has spared the Republic.

The picture of those days in 1930 is indeed tragic and horrible. Those were days of anxiety, confusion and uncertainty, with domestic strife added, enough to make anyone despair, especially in view of the fact that the struggle against so chaotic a situation had to be waged with a shaky budget that was cut in half, and with only the most meager funds.

The State was truly in desperate straits and there was no time to be lost before making extreme sacrifices. Would it, perchance, have been possible to control the chaos with measures attuned to the procedures of normal times? Halfway measures were quite out of the question. Drastic surgery was required. Instead of weakening or becoming discouraged, President Trujillo resolutely tackled the problems confronting his administration. With unflinching iron will, he undertook the trying task. Where cleaning out was necessary, it was done; rigid discipline was imposed to combat confusion and disorder; from the crumbling ruins there surged new buildings; everywhere his feverish activity multiplied itself, and the President directed even in its smallest detail the entire administration of public affairs. It was to be expected from Trujillo's dynamic character that quick, decisive steps would be taken to cope with the situation; there was indeed no reason to expect timorous, pusillanimous, half-hearted action that would only have made matters worse. He organized, rebuilt, brought tranquility wherever necessary. He cleaned the public Treasury of corruption, punishing harshly any defalcation, fraud or speculation, and gave the country the most honest adrinistration in its history. He cut budgetary expenditures by more than one fourth, and thus prevented what had seemed an inevitable deficit. He paid all government salaries and expenses promptly. The country's credit was raised to undreamed-of heights. Public funds were protected from the machinations of the so-called Generals, and thus the evil of petty partisan leadership was discouraged. Bureaucratic idleness as well as the lucrative contracts for a favored few were abolished, and thus corrupt parasitical practices were no more. As soon as the house had been put in order by means of those drastic measures which many have deemed impolitic, and the situation had been eased, he devoted all his attention to finding a permanent solution for the chaotic condition of the public Treasury and to obtain less onerous and more humane terms for repayment of the country's foreign debt.

President Trujillo is the only chief executive ever to seek conscientiously a solution for the Dominican Republic's financial problems with his heart full of hope for the country's redemption and with a truly crear understanding of the importance of his mission. Through an irony of fate, he is precisely that President who has had to fight against the most vicious world-wide financial crisis ever experienced.

Far from cowering at the size of the problem and at the alarming growing scarcity of resources, President Trujillo put into play everything through all available means. The struggle which he waged quietly without any fanfare was not without its bitter setbacks and disappointments, but eventually it was crowned with success and brought freedom to his people.

It would be an error bordering on grave injustice to view the rigurous organization and strict economy which President Trujillo imposed upon the public treasury as merely an ordinary accomplishment of a financier or the working of cool, calculated statesmanship. It was that and more. It was as much a labor of love as it was an achievement of his intellect; it was a feat made possible by his active and watchful patriotism.

It was not simply an efficient handling of figures that brought success. Rather, it was his unshakable determination, his tenaciousness, the unimpeachable honesty in the handling of public funds that won the day. The freedom he gained for his country had its roots deep in our supreme aspiration as an independent nation—freedom without restrictions, an unqualified sovereignty, honor without a single blemish.

As proof of the efficacy of the hard battle he waged to completely reorganize public administration it would be sufficient to point out, with patriotic pride, that all the expense budgets of President Trujillo's administration have provided surpluses, after prompt payment of all the items therein.

The ever greater increase in public revenues, due primarily to the country's astonishing progress which has been made possible by the peace he has imposed and scrupulous handling of public monies, may be understood from the prodigious fact that while in 1931 revenues totalled $7,350,000, the budget for 1951 amounted to $74,606,200, a figure more than ten times the national budget of twenty years ago!

The Dominican Republic is the only country in the world that may pride itself in having had, in the midst of the worst crisis ever seen, unfailing surpluses from its national budget —truly an outstanding achievement. All of this has been due solely to the direct personal efforts of President Trujillo, without foreign aid, without any Improvement Company, without anyone like Hollander, without any Mr. Dawes.

The contracts and treaties she had entered into with foreign boundholders had made the Dominican Republic's finances primarily a question of sovereignty. No matter the size thereof, no foreign debt can of itself imply the humiliating subjugation of a sovereign State. In fact, it may even cause it to prosper, provided there is not granted to a foreign power as a guarantee for its indebtedness any political intervention or administrative control as happened in the case of our country.

Albeit in brief fashion, it is worthwhile to look into the winding history of our foreign debt.

The first loan, the Hartmont loan, was contracted under President Buenaventura Báez in 1869. From 1888 to 1899, under President Heureaux, several loans, all impinging upon our national sovereignty, were arranged with Westerndorp and Company, increasing our indebtedness to $20,000,000. United States participation began with the transfer of the Westendorp contracts to the Santo Domingo Improvement Company, a New York firm. At no time had the Republic paid either the interest nor the money for amortization stipulated in those usurious contracts. The party holding power limited its efforts to obtaining, at any and all costs and subscribing whatever terms might be required, the money it sought; the obligation to pay was left for ensuing administrations to cope with.

Naturally enough, the national debt soared and the claims by bondholders became increasingly stronger. The expedient used was a new loan to consolidate the existing foreign debt, and the extortionate clauses ever became tougher; the Republic had to deliver into alien hands, as a guarantee, larger segments of its administrative autonomy.

After Heureaux's death, a $20,000,000 loan was obtained. It was from that moment on that the United States officially took a hand in the matter. Under the provisional government of Monsignor Adolfo A. Nouel a further loan of $1,500,000 was contracted. The Military Government of the American Occupation effected several loan operations in the guise of being a Dominican Government, one for

$5,000,000 for the payment of claims and another for $500,000 at a rate of interest of seven percent per year. In 1922 it issued bonds in the amount of $10,000,000. Under General Horacio Vásquez' administration the nation's indebtedness again reached the sum of $20,000,000.

In 1905 an agreement had been concluded with the United States for the settlement of pending debts and claims by means of a protocol providing for our Customs, which had previously been put up as a guarantee for the bondholders, to be operated by American officials directly appointed by the President of the United States. This treaty was drafted and put into effect by President Roosevelt, that is, the President Roosevelt of the imperialist era. The pretext he alleged was our non-payment of the interest and capital that comprised the Dominican Republic's public debt, which non-payment had caused persistent diplomatic representations in behalf of the bondholders the majority of whom were Belgian, Italian and French, a fact that, it was speciously argued, might involve the United States in complications with European nations which would conflict with the Monroe Doctrine should they attempt to employ for purposes of collection, in keeping with an old custom, the guns on their warships. The real underlying cause, however, was the expansion of Yankee trade and influence in the Caribbean area. The draft Treaty was rejected by the United States Senate that was then beginning to oppose President Theodore Roosevelt's policy of expansion, but he adopted its general lines for the Modus Vivendi that, without need of Senate approval, was put into effect as a provisional measure in April of that same year.

In 1907 a Convention between the United States and the Dominican Republic along the lines of the former one was approved, and by virtue thereof the administration of our Customs passed contractually into the hands of the United States and we assented, moreover, under Clause III of the Convention, to the following two limitations of our sovereignty: not to increase our public debt, and not to make any laws regarding customs duties without prior consent from the United States Government.

It must be pointed out that it was this unfortunate Clause III that later afforded the pretext for President Wilson, in turn, to order the military occupation of our country in 1916, as became evident from Note No. 14, dated November 19, 1915 addressed by United States Minister W. W. Russell, whose threatening terms stated, "The failure to comply with the provisions of the Budget, the fact that sums are voted in excess of probable revenues, the purchase of funds, supplies and materials for the payment of which there is no provision, are all regarded by the Department of State as contraventions of Clause III of the Convention". (1) In his note the Minister demanded:

a) The establishment of a Financial Advisor to compel compliance with Clause III; and

b) The creation of a Civil Guard commanded by American officers, "wherefor the Dominican Government undertook —for the preservation of internal peace, the security

---

(1) **Translator's note:** This text is a re-translation of a Spanish version, and not a verbatim copy of the original.

of individual rights and complete compliance with the provisions of the Convention— to create the same without delay and to maintain it." (1) A year later, the proclamation explaining the American intervention and military occupation stated: "Whereas the [Dominican] government has violated the said article III on more than one occasion... now, therefore, I, H. S. Knapp, Captain, United States Navy, do declare and proclaim to all concerned that the Dominican Republic is hereby placed under Military Occupation." (2).

In 1924 the Convention was revised to increase the indebtedness to $25,000,000, extending its term but leaving in full force the provisions that impinged upon our sovereignty, the pusillanimous revision in itself being otherwise of scarce importance.

This is the reason why the mere readjustment of the nation's indebtedness which President Trujillo brought about after the promulgation of his redeeming Emergency Law, though containing less burdensome and fairer conditions, and notwithstanding the fact that its achievement required great statesmanship and an iron will, fell short of fulfilling President Trujillo's own patriotic aspirations. He felt that the humiliating, vexing clauses of the Convention had to be abrogated altogether. This task which had seemed to all the preceding governments impossible and therefore undeserving of any attempt, was undertaken by Trujillo with righteous determination.

---

(1) Re-translated, as text referred to in preceding footnote.

(2) See Appendix I. The words quoted above are a re-translation.

It was a difficult situation. We found ourselves in a truly vicious circle, inasmuch as in order to obtain more favorable terms it was necessary to grant our consent to a prolonged extension, of several years' duration, of the existing provisions. However, President Trujillo was not discouraged. Instead of contenting himself —as the most optimistic persons held he should— with a modification of the onerous provisions that should render them more in keeping with our character as a country with the right to self-determination, he capitalized on the change of men and ideas that had taken place in Washington, and he channeled his persistent efforts toward obtaining complete abrogation of the Convention between the Dominican Republic and the United States. After seemingly endless, difficult and painfully drawn-out negotiations he attained his purpose with the signing of the Trujillo-Hull Treaty establishing the complete restoration of our country's unqualified sovereignty in financial matters. On July 17, 1947 —truly a red-letter day in our history— in a magnificent gesture President Trujillo paid off our foreign debt in its entirety, to the cent. He did this with an incredible daring and sense of responsibility more than twenty years before the date of its legal expiration. At one fell swoop Trujillo righted all the unforgivable mistakes of earlier administrations, including those in Washington and the government of the American Military Occupation itself. Rising to heights equal to those attained by the Founding Fathers of our country, Trujillo was able to say that the Republic was henceforth once again "absolutely free, absolutely independent and absolutely sovereign".

The Trujillo-Hull Treaty and the total payment of our foreign debt are landmarks in our history that have earned Generalissimo Trujillo the permanent title of Restorer of our Financial Independence, which was conferred upon him by our Congress with the enthusiastic support of all Dominicans.

The Greatest Need of the Nation is Order

Rafael L. Trujillo

CHAPTER XIV

ORGANIZATION OF THE NATIONAL ARMY

On December 18, 1918 Rafael L. Trujillo Molina received his appointment as a second Lieutenant in the Dominican National Guard, the country's army. That day marks the beginning of his military career; the story of that career was to become the history of the National Army which he later organized and brought to its present high peak of development, quality and efficiency.

The former National Army —if one may call an army that group of untrained men, in crowded unsanitary barracks, who only occasionally collected their rations from the government and who were armed with obsolete carbines — defies description indeed. A platoon consisted of soldiers who had been pressed into service, thrust into blue uniforms, dragged to the ranks by dint of saber blows without a medical examination and miserably shod. The "National Army" consisted of many such platoons, absolutely devoid of administrative technique, scientific instruction, discipline or basic training, other than what was absolutely necessary in order to parade on national holidays. Its total strength amounted to two battalions.. Inadequate rations, a total lack of hygiene and medical attention, ill treatment and cruel punishments made every soldier a potential deserter. At the first opportunity that presented itself, either in war or in peace, the men would go A.W.O.L. in search of better conditions. Barracks life was so hard and undesirable that desertions were constant and innumerable notwithstanding the terrible punishments meted out to those who were caught.

The troops were recruited from among the dregs of society, and were for the most part unemployed farm laborers, professional idlers, or village bullies without any education or social contacts with their fellow men, who had not yet acquired any habits of cleanliness and personal hygiene.

Being a soldier was like having the plague. Advance word that conscripts were to be drawn from a given section of the country was the signal for a general exodus. This regrettable state of affairs continued virtually unchanged for nearly seventy-five years throughout successive administrations.

In all justice, it must be admitted that President Heureaux did improve the Army somewhat, with regard to its uniforms and equipment. Krupp cannons were imported, and new instruments were obtained for the Army Band. A navy began to take shape with the purchase of three cruisers. European technicians arrived to train the soldiers and sailors. But the basic human element, which was the worst, remained unchanged. Upon the death of President Heureaux, even that sketchy organization vanished. The ships were either lost or sold, and the military equipment that had been purchased so dearly, and which the soldiers had not yet learned to handle, only served to add abundant fuel to our constant revolutionary holocausts, and the so-called National Army reverted to its perennial shoddiness, disorder, filth and chaos.

It was so disorganized that the different commissioned grades had lost all prestige, had no true military importance and commanded neither consideration nor respect. In those days it was easier to obtain the rank of Captain, Major or Colonel than it is to obtain that of Rural Marshal nowadays. Among the nations of the world, we were unrivalled in the number of Generals we possessed. We shattered all records in the Western Hemisphere, with the exception of Haiti, our only serious competitor. It was truly amazing how a civilian could acquire overnight the highest military rank, but there was a system to it. Graded promotions were non-existent. Any leader of a rebel band would simply promote himself to the rank of General, and if his side won, the Government would immediately confirm his rank officially. Thus rewarded, the machete-wielding rebel reigned supreme.

Of the many blessings derived by the nation from Trujillo's complete organization of the Army, one of the greatest has been the abolition of the mail-order Generals who were a disturbing element. They have disappeared, as if by magic. Formerly they were the ringleaders of revolutions. Today they may be seen peacefully ploughing fields, driving trucks or automobiles, working on sugar plantations or as foremen on road gangs.

During the American occupation, the Military Government devoted its best efforts to the creation of a militarized Civil Guard or National Police, which later served as a cadre for our Army. In 1918, 2nd Lieutenant Rafael L. Trujillo Molina joined that national Guard's select officer corps.

He was described as "a man free from vices and devoted to his work" by former Colonel Rafael A. Espaillat in biographical data which he published in 1935. Undoubtedly his temperate habits contributed greatly to his success. From the very outset, Trujillo's dynamic activities revealed his organizing ability, leadership, extraordinary administrative capacity and unbounded energy. He was a strong and severe commander, but he was fair; by showing no favoritism in the case of any of his relatives or friends, he soon earned unquestionable authority to mete out punishment to others. That is why the platoon he led as a Lieutenant, his company as a Captain, his battalion when he was a Major and the regiment he commanded as a Colonel were always pointed out as model units.

On November 10, 1920 his commanding officer had this to say of Trujillo, "I regard this officer as one of the best in the service". The following year, on March 31, 1921, another of his superiors, in reporting on an encounter with a guerrilla patrol, rated Trujillo thus, "His conduct before as well as during the encounter was outstanding. This officer has rendered excellent and highly valuable services." That is the record as stated in official documents, and such was the fame that surrounded the real creator of our Army.

In accordance with its aims, the American Military Government established in 1916, created a Police Force or National Guard, organized along modern lines of military efficiency, scientific training and rigid discipline. Although from its very beginning it lacked the essential characteristics of a real army, it did train real soldiers.

In the latter part of 1921, Trujillo entered the Training School at Haina and he graduated from it with honors. Thereafter, without a single interruption, his military career followed its brilliant course.

During those early years, the young officer's mind had room for but one thought: the complete organization of the Army. When finally, after long years of patient waiting, he became Commander-in-Chief on June 22, 1925, the Army was in wretched shape and fell far short of Trujillo's aspirations and ideals.

The same former Colonel Espaillat we have already quoted, who was at that time a member of the armed forces, goes on to say in his article with reference to the deplorable condition of the Army, that it "was falling apart, and its discipline as well as sense of duty were as empty words", and also that the condition in which Trujillo "found that institution was disastrous indeed." The task that lay before him was truly a difficult and thankless one.

It was not a job to be accomplished overnight. It required a good deal of time, but his perseverance was inexhaustible. Patience was necessary, and in him it was not wanting for a single moment. Energy was necessary; he had it in abundant measure. Finally, overcoming bitter disappointments and discouraging obstacles, he managed to replace chaos with order, and confusion and disorder with rigid discipline.

Anyone familiar with Trujillo knows that he is not one to content himself with half-way measures. Just as he demands of himself a strict compliance with duty, likewise he makes the same demand of others. He resolved to give solid training to the soldiers, to instruct them carefully in military science, to really teach them how to handle their weapons, ingraining the strictest military discipline in them. He succeeded completely. This achievement, in a negative and pessimistic milieu such as ours, was truly incredible. Everything had to be created from scratch, or else had to be completely changed over to a new gear. New men were needed, and when domestic sources failed to provide those with adequate qualifications he imported them from abroad. He also sent Dominicans abroad for specialized training. Camp life was one exercise after another, one job after another. And so it went on, day after day. It was a question of hammering on a hard anvil, overcoming difficulties, rewarding the good and discarding deadwood. That is how our Army was forged, and such is the spirit that inspires it.

Anyone who compares our splendid, well-organized and disciplined Army with the small and wretched force that Trujillo fell heir to in 1925 must surely believe in miracles. Its transformation has been so tremendous that it is incredible.

It is obvious that in order to work such a miracle President Trujillo must have possessed extraordinary virtues such as a professional skill, experience, leadership, organizing ability, and tremendous will-power. Only a man who knew the Army as the palm of his own hand, and one who had studied both in theory and in practice its complete organization from a squad all the way up to a full division and who was acquainted intimately and thoroughly, as the Generalissimo is, with the psychology of the soldier, his habits and his failings, his aspirations and ideals, could have obtained such splendid results. The most notable part of it is that Trujillo has accomplished that huge task without contracting any loans, as Heureaux did, and, quite the contrary, paying off at the same time the debts assumed by earlier administrations.

Our Army, composed of strong, healthy, clean, well trained men, commanded by a brilliant staff of officers who would be a credit to any country, is today a source of national pride. It is one of Trujillo's most finished works, and that into which he has poured the greatest measure of devotion.

The Army knows all these things. It is aware of his worries and efforts for the individual soldier's wellbeing, for his enjoyment of an adequate mess and comfortable quarters, for the preservation of his health, for his entertainment. It knows the paternal regard Trujillo has for its members, and they reciprocate it with a loyalty and admiration that has been seldom equalled. The Army and Trujillo, intimately linked as they are, form a closely bound whole, inseparable and indestructible. Trujillo has instilled his own spirit in our military men.

Wherever one finds an officer or other member of our Army, be it an aristocratic salon, on the street, in a café or in barracks, the impression one invariably gets is that of an educated and proper person who always acts as is his duty and who is constantly aware of his obligation to honor the institution of which he is a member.

On several occasions famous components of foreign armies have paraded through the streets and avenues of our capital city, with wonderful precision, to the tune of stirring marches. Along the same streets and avenues our own Army has paraded and its martial bearing as well as the mathematical precision of its movements, under the folds of our glorious flag, have never failed to win the most favorable comparison with those foreign units.

The admiration, enthusiasm and sympathy that the population feels for our Army is due primarily to the deep conviction shared by all —whether big or small, natives or foreigners— that it is, under Trujillo's aegis, the real cause and guarantee of the order and blessed peace our country enjoys. The people have a feeling of trust when they see it. They feel supported, guarded and preserved. That feeling which our people have for the Army is not only visible in the loud cheers that greet its members on parade, but also in the affectionate consideration, respect and regard with which they are treated in their contacts with the public.

The Secretary of State for War, Navy and Aviation, General Héctor B. Trujillo Molina, is the head of our National Army. He has been President Trujillo's intelligent, efficient and untiring helper in organizing the Armed Forces of the Republic. Having been trained and guided by him, General Héctor B. Trujillo Molina is so closely identified with his great brother, so linked to his fate and his wondrous achievements as a statesman that it would be impossible to imagine another person fully as much in touch with his lofty aims and so perfectly imbued with the spirit of his patriotic mission. Honest, studious, competent, with a quiet nature, fair in his judgments, the enormous experience he has acquired over so many years with the President constitutes a truly precious asset. He enrolled in the Army as a Private on March 1, 1926. Grade by grade, he rose from the ranks on his own merits and as a reward for his industry, exemplary conduct and devotion to duty. On July 1, 1930 he was commissioned an officer, with the grade of Second Lieutenant. In 1936 he was designated Chief of Staff and promoted to Brigadier General. In September of 1941 he became Major General. On November 11, 1944 he was appointed Secretary of State for War and Navy as well as Commander in Chief of the National Army, with the rank of full General. As Secretary for War, Navy and Aviation, an office he has held with admirable efficiency already for more than six years, General Héctor B. Trujillo Molina is First Vice President of the Republic under the provisions of our Constitution. In the discharge of his office, which requires unqualified confidence, General Trujillo has fully measured up, loyally and efficiently, to all the hopes and the trust the Generalissimo places in him.

The National Army comprises at present the following arms: Infantry, Artillery, Cavalry, Air Force, Signal Corps, and Navy. It has, besides, the following services: Quartermaster General, Medical Corps, and Judge Advocate General's.

Each branch of the Army is under a General Staff.

The General Staff of the National Army consists of a Chief of Staff, a Deputy Chief of Staff, and an Adjutant to General Headquarters, in charge of Personnel and Orders.

Specialized Services:

General Headquarters of the Army Company; Adjutants General Corps; Aviation Company; Presidential Guard; Signal Company; Headquarters Musical Band.

Medical Corps:

1 Medical Colonel, Director of the Medical and Militatary Sanitation Corps; 1 Major, Director of "Profesor Marion" Hospital; 1 Dentist Major, in charge of the Dentistry Section; 1 Captain, National Army, Administrative Officer of "Profesor Marión" Hospital; 1 Medical Captain, cardiologist; 1 Medical Captain, urologist; 1 Captain, pharmacist; 4 Medical Captains; 1 First Lieutenant, Medical Corps Quartermaster; 3 Medical First Lieutenants; 1 First Lieutenant, pharmacist; 2 Medical Second Lieutenants; 2 Second Lieutenants, dentists; 1 Second Lieutenant, assistant; 4 Cadets, several Sergeants, Corporals and Privates. In addition, it has the services of several civilian specialists, 27 nurses and other helpers.

Office of Materiel:

Headquarters Company, Office of Materiel; Ordnance Company.

Quartermaster General, Armed Forces:

Quartermaster Company; Transportation Battalion.

Training Headquarters Company:

Training Headquarters Company: 1 Director of Training; 1 Adjutant to the Director of Training.

Military District:

1 Commander of the Military District, National Army; 1 Adjutant to the Commander of the Military District.

First Brigade, National Army:

1 Commander of the First Brigade, National Army; 1 Adjutant to the Commander of the First Brigade, N. A.; 1 Headquarters Company, First Brigade, N. A.

Second Brigade, National Army:

1 Commander of the Second Brigade, National Army; 1 Adjutant of the Second Brigade, N. A.; 1 Headquarters Company, Second Brigade, N. A.; 1 Musical Band of the Fourth Regiment; 1 Cavalry troop.

The Navy

The General Staff of the Navy consists of the following:

1 Chief of Staff; 1 Deputy Chief of Staff; 1 Chief of the Office of Artillery and Coast Defense; 1 Chief of the Office of Naval Construction and Repair; 1 Quartermaster General of the Navy; 1 Chief of the Intelligence and Signal Office; 1 Chief of the Hydrographic and Coastal Buoy Office;

1 Chief of the Medical and Sanitary Corps; 1 Chief of the Office of Auxiliary Forces.

The navy maintains two Naval Bases. One, in Ciudad Trujillo, is the headquarters for the following organizations:

a) Headquarters Detachment; b) Auxiliary Forces Detachment; c) Signal Section of the Navy; d) Naval Artillery Section; e) Naval Section "A"; Naval Section "B"; g) Naval Section "D"; h) Naval Section "F"; i) Naval Section "G"; j) Naval Quartermaster Section; k) Naval Lighthouses and Buoys Section.

In addtion, there is a Seamanship School and the Naval Academy located at Sans Souci.

The Naval Base at Las Calderas includes the following organizations:

a) Naval Section "C"; b) Naval Section "E".

The following Offices are also based there:

a) Office of Naval Construction and Repair; b) Docks Numbers 1 and 2; c) Departamental Quartermaster.

Navy Dock Number 3 is located in San Pedro de Macorís.

Dominican Air Force:

The General Staff of the Dominican Air Force consists of the following:

a) Chief of Staff; b) Deputy Chief of Staff; c) Operations Department; d) Mechanics and Transportation Department; e) Alignment Department; f) Weapons Department; g) Radio and Signal Department; h) Personnel and Orders

Department; i) Chief of the School of Aviation; j) Air Force Quartermaster; k) Medical Corps, Dominican Air Force.

Thus organized, equipped and trained, the magnificent National Army that President Trujillo created and formed is fulfilling the mission entrusted to it by our Constitution and laws to safeguard the maintenance of national peace and to protect our country against all foreign agression.

In addition to discharging faithfully this basic mission, our Army renders valuable cooperation to several other branches of the Government, particularly the Police, Communications, Public Health and Agriculture, contributing in an effective manner to maximum efficiency.

Prior to the American Military Occupation, United States diplomacy insisted upon ascribing to the Dominican Government all blame for the administrative confusion and the political unrest then prevalent. One of the Occupation's principal and persistent objectives was the formation of a Civil Guard or National Police Force that would guarantee internal security and maintain peace. To that end in 1915 it demanded, threateningly, together with financial control over our Treasury, acceptance of an American Military Commission with full powers to establish, train and direct a Guard or Police Corps which, although drawing its pay from money from the pockets of Dominican citizens, would be commanded by United States officers.

They demanded the Treasury and the Army, forever our two vulnerable points and a double vacuum in our organization as a free and independent nation through which

American imperialist intervention was able to infiltrate. The strict and honest organization of our Treasury and the scientific modernization of our Army must therefore be viewed as not merely the work of a genius in statesmanship but, primarily and essentially, as a keystone in the fabric erected by Trujillo's farsighted and abiding patriotism.

CHAPTER XV

A PERMANENT BOUNDARY

President Trujillo has fulfilled to the utmost the deepest and most paramount aspirations of the Dominican people. He has solved definitely their most urgent national problems; he has allayed their gravest fears, and he has brought about the recovery of their depleted vitality. Above all, he has given them new faith in themselves — faith in their historic destiny, faith in their future. He has made over the country from the turbulent, backward and poor nation that it was but a few years ago into the orderly, peaceful, progressive and prosperous country it is today. Today, the Republic is a small but educated, hospitable and worthy nation, peaceful and hard-working, revitalized by peace, wholly refashioned in the mold of the civilized progress that has spread throughout the land.

Of all the problems faced by the Republic from the day it was founded, the most vital and acute as well as the most difficult and hazardous was unquestionably the old problem of its boundary. It struck at the very roots of our existence as a nation, and it was a veritable nightmare for the Dominican people. From the distant days of European colonización, it was a constant source of worry for the rulers of the Spanish portion of the island.

The problem of Haiti was never merely a question of a frontier, but rather, as Señor Peña Batlle rightly stated in his speech in the border town of Elías Piña, a problem of neighborliness. The peoples mistrusting each other, separated by different traditions and different ways of life, unacquainted with one another and without social contact, one of them being more densely populated and more aggresive than the other, it never proved easy to find a solution to the question of how to delimit their common boundary and to their sharing the same island. The problem goes back to the times of the buccaneers. Spanish and French history during the seventeenth and eighteenth centuries is filled with incidents stemming therefrom. And we, as an independent nation, acquired that problem along with our political freedom. Wise men in Europe as well as learned men of good will in either country endeavored to find a remedy. Several treaties were concluded — the Treaty of Aranjuez in 1777, the Treaty of Basle in 1795, and the Treaties between the Dominican Republic and Haiti in 1874, 1899 and 1929.

The boundary question was becoming more annoying with each passing day, causing fear and alarm among our people and injuring their pride which already had suffered on previous occasions to such an extent that many a patriotic citizen felt, before the Treaty of 1936 was concluded between the two countries, that it would never be definitely solved unless it were by new recourse to war.

Our fears were not unfounded. Many were the attempted invasions that the Dominicans were forced to throw back at various times in their history by sheer dint of their fighting ability.

Neither the majesty of the law nor the justice of our cause were enough in themselves to safeguard us against constant aggression by our western neighbors. That ever present dread weighed heavily upon the Dominicans to such an extent that it carried them to the border of despair, and in bygone eras it undermined the patriotism of many illustrious leaders who lost faith in the Republic's stability and were led — despite the fact that they had generously shed their blood for the preservation of its freedom— to seek a remedy for the situation under the folds of foreign flags.

We are generally inclined to reproach bitterly the action of those of our forebears who lost faith in their country, guiding ourselves by the biased opinion of writers who were their contemporaries, without analyzing the social and political conditions that may have influenced their decisions. In thinking of the Dominican Republic one should not conjure in one's mind the platonic ideal of a model republic. Switzerland is free from any threat from Haiti, and she is likewise exempt from ethnic and atavistic factors that have contributed to our character and our thinking. We should ever bear in mind that the earliest measures we adopted as a nation were decisively influenced by the Haitian factor. The project for a French protectorate, union with Colombia, Spanish annexation or Yankee annexation —these were all different phases of one and the same idea, one and the same dread: Haitian invasion.

Trujillo' s advent to power changed the picture altogether. It took him no time to realize that it was not merely a question of drawing a boundary line hither or yon, and that, besides, the threat of invasion —be it armed or peaceful— by our western neighbors had to be solved. With characteristic determination he set himself to finding a solution to the problem.

In his brilliant work **La Cuestión de Límites** ("The Boundary Question"), Dr. García Mella describes the condition in which both Dominicans and Haitians lived prior to 1930, as follows:

"Less in need of land than our neighbors were, with a rather scant population, our frontiers have remained almost deserted. This, together with the internal problems that unfailingly absorbed our national administrations, made possible, first, the continual advance, which went unnoticed, of Haitian settlers who could not be expelled inasmuch as they did not challenge the nation's domain, and, subsequently, the establishment of Haitian authorities in each small population center, effected clandestinely if necessary. Trade furthered their purposes. The great distances separating the southwestern frontier regions from the principal Dominican commercial centers, the state of disrepair of the roads linking the country's towns, the proximity of important Haitian commercial centers and, particularly, the positive assurance of an outlet for their sales, free from all contingencies, made our frontier communities tributaries of the Haitian cities."

In order to understand well the heights that unlimited Haitian ambition had reached and the Haitians' aggressive purposes which went entirely beyond reason and fairness, it should suffice to know that many years after the Dominican Republic had won its independence the Haitian Constitution proclaimed, as a permanent challenge, that its territory's sole boundary was the sea. That country sought many times to fulfill its arrant ambition, invading our territory with large armed forces. The latter's march through each succeeding Dominican town invariably left in its wake blood, fire and devastation.

Later on, with the passing of time, the defeat inflicted upon the Haitians on the battlefields caused this type of armed invasion to cease, and it became the peaceful, surreptitious, hushed invasion that we endured until recent times —a gradual taking over by "fifth columns" of lands and towns that were unquestionably and by right ours alone. Protected by our cordiality and circumventing our immigration restrictions, more than 100,000 Haitians from the lowest strata of society —for cultured Haitians emi grate only to France— invaded our farm lands, our valleys and our hills. They infiltrated into the huts of our peasants, our sugar plantations, the villages and towns, the workshops; into our very homes, replacing our peons, workmen and domestic servants, performing all sorts of work for unfairly competing wages and lowering our standard of living, degenerating our language and our customs, filling our highways and our byways with beggars, introducing savage rites and exotic heresies, with succeeding administrations in our country patiently looking on and no one nor anything apparently capable of halting the shadow cast by their invasion.

It need not be surprising, therefore, that such a state of affairs should have bore discord, jealousy and suspicion, and that there were sporadic bloody clashes. On several occasions the public spirit of Dominicans was disturbed by military preparations for invasion or actual threats of invasion by Haiti. During the Cáceres administration we nearly came to grips. Unrest and friction were caused by the frequent stealing of cattle and the furtive depredations of property by Haitian marauders who went unpunished. That is why there have been several border incidents.

The events of 1937, which were so misinterpreted in certain foreign sectors for lack of adequate information on what had transpired before, constitute one of those typical cases shared by the peoples of both countries that unfortunately have taken place for centuries. Another incident took place in 1941. The Dominican Government's energetic attitude moved the Haitian Government to make a thorough investigation this time. The result was the irrefutable document by the Secretary of the Interior in the Haitian President's Cabinet, M. Elie Lescot, (1) establishing, with

(1) Elie Lescot, before becoming President of Haiti, was, first, his country's Minister to the Dominican Republic, and later he was transferred to Washington in the same capacity. During that period he showed a great deal of sympathy and friendship for the Dominican people and for President Trujillo, from whom he requested and obtained other favors as well as money on various occasions. As soon as Lescot became President of Haiti he forgot his close friendship. Instead of gratitude he felt envy. Instead of devoting himself, from his high office, to reestablishing harmony and to promoting conciliation between the people of the two countries, as has been and shall ever be President Trujillo's unfailing desire, he unexpectedly, without having the slightest motive and not even a reasonable pretext, became overnight the bitterest foe of the Dominicans and their Chief Executive. But perhaps that sudden change

unmitigated frankness, the true facts of the case. On September 9, 1941 there was published in Port-au-Prince, Haiti, the following official communiqué.

Communiqué dated September 9, 1941 by the Department of the Interior

"Ministers Noel and Rouzier have returned from their mission in the North. Their preliminary report to President Lescot sets forth that they have verified the existence of real bands of marauders who, after having stolen livestock on Dominican territory, come to sell it in Haiti, which frequently gives rise to serious incidents between these marauders and the farmers who defend their property. These activities are intolerable, the more so because it has been revealed that they are, for the most part, provoked by individuals who are interested in creating friction between the two governments, to such an extent that some of them, whose domicile is not in the place where they resided, have taken flight immediately after the Haitian authorities arrived. Consequently, President Lescot has issued formal instructions for the whole weight of the law to be applied by the Haitian military authorities, acting in perfect agreement with the military authorities of the Dominican Republic, in order to put an end to the nefarious activities of these marauders". (2)

---

in his attitude was more apparent than real, notwithstanding his unctuous complacency and the masked disimulation of a false friendship, he may never have been at heart anything but a bitter enemy. Or who knows what Macbeth's witches may have whispered in his ear?

(2) See Appendix II.

President Trujillo tackled the frontier problem with patriotic inspiration, conscious of his responsibility as head of the nation, and he wasted no time in carrying out one of the most important if not the most trascendental of his brilliant deeds as a statesman. First, he brought down to definite terms and speeded up the negotiations that had been prolonged over decades to fix the boundary line along its very site. Second, he dictated the measures that were necessary in order to Dominicanize our side of the boundary. Since that day, not a single Haitian has crossed the frontier without complying with our immigrations laws. Trujillo imposed, inexorably, respect for the law and all that is Dominican.

Overnight, it may be said, President Trujillo transformed that entire region. He created new provinces so that the watchful eye of the authorities might never be distant; he established courts and built and made over whole towns, endowing them with modern public buildings, schools, irrigation canals and ample roads. He had farming tools and seeds distributed, and sent out teachers, along with pianos, orchestras and musical instructors to teach the children our anthem. He started special courses in Dominican history to inspire patriotism through the telling of the heroic feats that wrought our independence. He created agricultural colonies, sponsored new industries and extended protection to local trade so that the new settlers might avail themselves of it. He built new churches and sent missionary priests to preach and teach there the forgotten Gospel of Jesus. To each home located near the frontier he gave our flag which is emblazoned with the cross, so that all might know and learn to love and venerate that sacred symbol of our liberty. And he brought to that distant region our Spanish culture, our Christian ideals, the idea of our nationality and the emotions it awakens.

The Trujillo-Hull Treaty, whereby he gave back to our country the financial sovereignty it had lost, and the Treaty with Haiti, which made possible the Dominicanization of our frontier, rescuing a vast extent of territory that the neglect of earlier administrations had given up to the insatiable ambition of our neighbors, are two everlasting monuments to Trujillo's glory. With the former he put an end to the American meddling that dated from the imperialist era; with the other he ended once for all the pacific but illegal invasion by Haiti, drawing a permanent boundary that delimits in a fixed manner the respective jurisdiction of either country and leaves to each that portion of the earth where it is to fulfill, without molestation or fear, its God-given historical destiny.

CHAPTER XVI

TRUJILLO, CREATOR OF PEACE

It is said that peoples are forgetful; that the sorrows of the past, the tribulations of yesteryear, the penury and insecurity that caused so much bitterness and so many tears to be shed are soon forgotten in halcyon days. True. So they are, but not through indolence but, rather, because of that entirely human faculty of adjusting to improved conditions —to whatever may be good, pleasant or comfortable; to each new conquest of science; to all human progress: the railroad ,transatlantic liners, the telephone, radio, airplanes. Man quickly accustoms himself as though he had always enjoyed them.

The suffering, the former long journeys on horseback over the rough trails, the privations and anguish, the sudden fear that grips one on hearing gunfire, unwarranted imprisonments, tragic holocausts of so many precious lives —all these things are soon discarded from the memories of men as passing, temporary events that leave no wake behind. No matter how deep the wound may have been, hardly does a scar show. That prodigious faculty of recovery, of forgetting promptly, that individual men as well as nations have, is the subconscious working of optimism, which is innate in all humans and sets aside whatever may cause sorrow, spend our energy and undermine our strength. Hiding such things under a merciful forgetfulness, optimism enkindles in men the spark of undying hope.

Still, the Dominican nation in its present era of full exultation, great material progress and high moral elevation; in this period of thorough transformations wherein it develops its unquenchable vitality, undertakes the exploitation of untold wealth and devotes its efforts wholeheartedly to productive endeavors; in these times when, thanks to Trujillo, the country is spanned from one end to the other by fine highways, when its ocean ports have been perfected to the ultimate degree and the flow of its rivers has been diverted into new channels, its lands cleared, its agriculture made to burgeon, with its trade flourishing, its population growing by leaps and bounds, its laws respected, order firmly established and peace secured, still the Dominican nation has not forgotten that dread period, those terrible years of unutterable suffering. It has not lost its memory of those anguished days when guns cracked at the crossways, when imprisonment was arbitrary and when internecine war unleashed its full fury. The nation well remembers how the sword would strike down all attempts at progress and order; how the workman's machete became a campaign weapon; how the earth was not plowed to produce men's sustenance but to receive their bodies; how the fields languished uncultivated for lack of the manpower engaged in fighting; how there was no encouragement to work, for the products of labor were at the mercy of the first armed guerrilla to lay hands upon them; how no one enjoyed security, guarantees of any kind, tranquility, faith or peace.

No, the Dominican people have not forgotten. Nor can they ever grow oblivious to those tragic, painful years when they suffered every conceivable martyrdom —their country invaded, their sovereignty truncated, their flag defiled, their soil impoverished. That is why their appreciation, their love and their devotion to Trujillo are unbounded. Their gratitude to him is immense. Because Trujillo gave them peace.

The Dominican people have had many opportunities for showing Generalissimo Trujillo the faith they have in him as well as their unalterable loyalty to the principles which he defends and embodies. Never, however, has that regard been more evident than in the elections held in 1938. It was a term for which Trujillo had refused to run, despite a unanimous request by his Party. The people were deeply touched and became alarmed, for they took his refusal to mean that he would forever remain away from government and politics. In compact, enthusiastic crowds burning with fervor; in endless marching lines of women; in the four walls of their homes; by apprehensive comments on the street; by hushed prayers; in the workshops, through the press, on speakers' stands, in every manner in which they could express their desires, their aspirations and their hopes, the Dominican people declared their wish that Trujillo continue as President of the Republic. In the highest circles as well as in the most humble homes; in aristocratic clubs as much as in the most out-of-the-way neighborhoods; alike among the professional classes as among workingmen, in the University as well as in the rural schools, in all the manifestations of this pulsating earth, people of all ages, from children to the aged, the cry of all, the thoughts of all and the will of all—resolved, uncontainable and unbreakable— was this: Trujillo must continue as President.

A similar case is now taking place. The next electoral campaign is still two years away, and already the people are declaring themselves insistently in favor of his reelection which today is even more essential and justified than before, not only because of the serious problems, dangers and difficulties that the country still has before it in the post-war era but because of the increasing and terrible menace to our institutions and way of life which Communism presents, problems that the people believe only Trujillo will be able to tackle and overcome.

The spontaneous demonstrations of solidarity for his reelection that have been held by businessmen, industrialists, professional men, workers and farmers are the living expression of deeply popular anxiety. The Dominican people believe in Trujillo alone.

This is so because they have in Trujillo an asset of inestimable worth such as few countries have in these trying times. His broad knowledge of all branches of the administration; the vast experience he acquired during more than twenty years directing public affairs; the respect that his subordinates have for him, which is a mixture of the affection, admiration and fear one might have toward a just father; the burning enthusiasm his presence awakens among the masses of the people; his intimate knowledge of those who in one way or another have a hand in politics (friends or enemies, Dominicans or foreigners); his thorough acquaintance with the land that he has visited from one corner to another on countless occasions, without excluding a single town; his profound and proven sense of fairness and his insight into his milieu, all these are precious things that no other Dominican now possesses and that none in the past ever had, and they are the reason why the country cannot do without him in forthcoming years.

The love, devotion and loyalty of the people for Trujillo stems primarily from the fact that they know, without need of anyone pointing it out to them, that it is to Trujillo alone that they owe their wellbeing, their prosperity, their tranquility and, above all, their peace.

It can be said quite appropriately that the country's peace has known no disturbance since Trujillo came to power. The two or three uprisings that took place in the early days of his first term and the recent attempted invasion at Luperón were circumscribed and localized to a small portion of its territory, and the enemy, surprised in his hideout, was surrounded and destroyed in less time than was formerly required by the Army's battalions to reach the forested hills where rebel bands hid. The inhabitants of the sections involved did not even interrupt their daily occupations. Outside the area of combat itself, the rest of the country remained peacefully quiet.

Any plots, cabals and rioting such as formerly existed now have been done away with by direct, uncompromising means right at the point where they originated, with lightning speed, at one fell swoop. Trujillo's strong arm has made itself felt.

The solid structure of Trujillo's peace has withstood all tests, as has been demonstrated whenever he has gone abroad for a long period of time, to travel in Europe and the United States, without there having been the least political disturbance —a rare sight indeed in Latin America.

This has been possible because Trujillo's Peace is not, as has been the case elsewhere, a peace imposed by force of arms. It is a thing that has cast deep roots in the spirit of the Dominican people. The peace which President Trujillo's patriotic efforts have maintained in the Republic is not solely the peace which the preservation of public order implies and which is a negative and sterile peace consisting only of the cessation of uprisings and intestine revolt without any eradication of the disturbing factors that are their cause. It is, rather, the beneficent and fruitful peace from which material and moral blessings flow for the worker; peace for the farmer who tills his soil and waits to harvest in security the fruits of his labors; peace for the workingman whose hours of work have diminished and whose wages have increased; peace for the honest citizen, for the father of a family, who devotes himself to his daily task without fear of any upheaval, without any other fear, in short, than a holy fear of God, the law and his own conscience; peace for Dominican women who, instead of weeping over the death and destruction of fratricidal wars, now find themselves raised from their former inferior position to the exalted and inspiring status of full citizens;

peace for minors as well as adults, who may now give themselves to the study of whatever sciences or arts they pursue or enjoy their favorite sports, without their minds being poisoned by partisan hatreds; peace for a whole nation that, after having broken the disgraceful fetters of the past, is now, at long past, in complete possession of its sovereignty, right up to its very frontiers, in full creative and progressive activity, its heart filled with enthusiasm and hope at the prospects of an alluring future.

The inestimable advantage that this internal peace which Trujillo has given the Republic and from which future generations will benefit to an even greater extent impose upon them as well as upon ourselves the grave and tremendous responsibility of preserving it by dint of any and all sacrifices that may be necessary, as a supreme, honored legacy. We must maintain and preserve it so that its countless, immense benefits which have made possible our present progress may become permanent, to the end that this glorious achievement by Trujillo may be perpetuated forever. May it be again said in the future, as Trujillo said on a memorable occasion, "The Dominican Republic is an absolutely sovereign nation!"

Blessed be a thousand times this Peace created by Trujillo, and eternal glory to the powerful hand that has brought it about!

CHAPTER XVII

COMMERCE IN THE CARIBBEAN

To focus adequately the serious problems of peace with a proper mental attitude it is necessary to think in terms of the whole world and to lay aside all selfish territorial ambitions as well as the urge toward self-aggrandizement at the expense of others, avoiding thus the awakening of bitter feelings, caused by lack of fairness, and the desire to right grievances, which is felt by peoples who are humiliated. For rapport to be established between hostile nations it is necessary to create first a climate of reciprocal tolerance, mutual understanding and altruistic renunciation, wherein both sides will be willing to shed the selfishness that makes them want justice only for themselves. One must live in keeping with the spirit of the times and discard old prejudices.

Hereafter equal justice is what must be the guiding principle in international relations, for respecting the right of others and granting them the consideration and understanding that one would demand for oneself is the way in which that golden biblical rule is to be applied among the nations, each helping itself by helping others.

That is the only way to attain the ideal mean between opposing tendencies, the consolidation of peace, the rule of justice, and the final liberation of mankind.

Only when that goal is reached will men be able to give themselves over to an unrestricted enjoyment of their freedom, under the protecting shadow of a social justice that will have banished want and all forms of slavery forever from the face of the earth. We will then have a nobler and a finer world in which life will be truly worth living, where intelligence will gain its due reward, work will be compensated in a fair and adequate manner, the doctrine of Jesus will be practiced and not merely preached, and equality —man's supreme ideal— will become a reality, with all barriers and prejudices abolished as a natural result of the rule of one language alone, one currency alone, one law alone, and one God alone.

The post-war era has created a new international law —that of the interdependence of nations. If the measures for collective security are to be safeguarded under that new law, each State must recognize its own subordination and the limitations upon its sovereignty. If the peace is to be a lasting one and if the freedom of men and the measures for social justice as well as for the unfettered development of the world's economy are to be achieved as permanent gains by mankind throughout all countries, the idea of the Nation-State's sovereignty as conceived by statesmen in the nineteenth and twentieth centuries will have to be radically modified. What is advantageous to the community, the rigths of all and the rule of justice have to take precedence over the selfish interest of each one alone. Nationalism gained force and popular support after the French Revolution, and it may be said that in mankind's evolution toward greater freedom for men it fulfilled its historical role, at least in the civilized parts of the earth. However, in the face of the modern concept of national sovereignty, the former is no longer the concept upon which international relations are based. The exploitation of natural resources, the progressive development of the idea of individual liberty and an ever greater respect for the just rights of labor undermined its foundations. State internationalism in turn has brought the new international law based upon the interdependence of nations. France again is the European country leading in this evolution of the concept of the modern State, through the Schuman Plan to pool the production, distribution and sale of all the steel and coal produced in France, Germany, Britain, the Netherlands and Belgium, and, later on, the steel and coal of all Europe. Harold Stassen, the American statesman already has expressed it when he remarked that absolute nationalism died with the advent of the airplane, radio and robot bombs. At least, as a political theory it has become obsolete, and politics wise that is the worst thing that can befall either men or ideas.

No matter how big and powerful, no nation may be regarded, strictly speaking, as absolutely independent in either a political or an economic sense. In one way or another, to a greater or lesser extent, each has depended upon others for the expansion of its commercial and industrial activities; for obtainning the raw materials it may lack or possesses in sufficient quantities; to maintain the high standard of living of its own population, and to succeed in defending itself against foreign aggression. The British need to import meat from Argentina, Uruguay and some of their colonies if they are to have that product in anything like sufficient quantity. And how would Americans and Europeans manage to drink coffee were it not for Brazil, Colombia, the Dominican Republic and Haiti? How would the United States Government manufacture atom bombs without uranium from the Congo?

Who would have thought that a few months after entering World War II so rich a country as the United States would see fifty percent of its vehicular traffic paralyzed due to gasoline and tire rationing, and that months after the war's end it would have to continue rationing coffee, sugar, meat and so many other essential products whose abundance was everywhere apparent? The savage attack upon Pearl Harbor closed the markets for rubber, quinine, jute and other raw materials that may be found in large quantities only on the other side of the Pacific, and caused very serious disturbances in American industry which was forced to produce substitutes for the articles the United States could no longer import.

The war more than clearly demonstrated the fallacy of American isolation and of the so-called splendid isolation of Britain as well as the futility of selfish French protective tariffs. In the post-war era, altruism will be a necessity among the governments of the world powers, rather than a virtue. If they have taken to heart the painful lessons of the last war, they will have to be tolerant, understanding and generous in their relations with weaker countries, not so much for the sheer sake of goodness but for calculated, selfish reasons.

The present general trend should be toward a well guided international cooperation whose ultimate goal will be to secure bilateral, regional, continental and world-wide agreements to reduce customs barriers to a minimum until, in so far as is feasible, their complete eradication is accomplished.

Notwithstanding the optimism and enthusiasm aroused by these happy prospects, one must not overlook the reality of present-day conditions which is by no means entirely rosy, for mankind travels slowly along the road of progress. The generation which is trying to cope with problems of peace against Communism's aims of world domination is the same generation that brought on the war, making that conflict possible through its errors, shortsightedness and lack of preparation. The protagonists are the same, with the same virtues and the same faults. Post-war hopes have foundered on the rocks of the financial power of vested interests, the selfishness of the privileged classes, the enormous political influence of the advocates of high protective tariffs, on the one hand, and the disruptive forces of Communism, on the other, in their eternal conflict. Common sense and sound judgment will ultimately prevail over the bickering between the supporters of free trade and the advocates of protective tariffs, for although mankind's centuries-old pursuit of progress is slow, it is relentless.

In the rivalry between commercial interests that will eventually develop once the world's economy is placed upon a sounder and more equitable basis, attempts will be made to reach a healthy equilibrium, bearing in mind primarily, for the distribution of reciprocal responsibility and advantages, the geographical location, the productive capacity and the purchasing power, both real and potential, of each country. A selfish, unilateral policy such as the one embodied in the Smoot-Hawley Tariff Act of the United States or the Ottawa agreements that were a reprisal against that Act and established a clause providing for treatment equal to that accorded the most favored nation, has now become unthinkable.

A far broader vision is now the guiding principle of activity in the international realm by the United States, Britain, France, Canada and the larger Latin American nations. The bilateral agreements for reciprocal trade sponsored by the United States, the Truman Doctrine and the Marshall Plan for the reconstruction of Europe —whose prime object is the lowering of economic barriers among neighboring nations on that continent—as well as the proposed customs union between France and Italy are measures and trends that allow one to predict for a not too distant future the post-war world's reconstruction along less selfish and more equitable lines.

This does not mean, of course, that the particular interests of each country would be laid aside. Undoubtedly, as world peace is agreed upon, each will acquire a given field for commercial activity, vast or of limited size according to whether its own resources are greater or lesser, in which field it may possibly want to obtain or maintain an already existing preponderant interest. Such special interests refer principally to those lands with a homogeneous language, culture and history.

Let us cite our own case as an example. Side by side with the general interest that the Dominican Republic has in world trade, as an independent nation, there is a special or particular interest, or, rather, a regional interest which refers to the geographic area wherein it is situated, which will come to the fore when the time comes for making commercial agreements. W refer to the Dominican Republic's essential interest in acquiring, within a framework whose stability will be guaranteed by treaties against all ulterior protectionist deceit, an important share in Caribbean trade.

There is no doubt that, in that wise and to achieve a quicker and more general expansion of trade among the lands comprising the West Indies, the ideal solution for us would be a customs union among the Caribbean islands, including the independent republics as well as the colonial territories, effected through a gradual adoption of measures tending to reduce import duties to a minimum and their eventual total extinction, as the only defense for the future against commercial absorption and the discriminatory practices of the great powers. The late war evinced the following truth: without the food products exported by the Dominican Republic many people in the islands of the West Indies would have succumbed to famine. It is therefore in the interest of all that that trade should be increased on a sound basis.

With statesmanlike wisdom, from the outset of his administration President Trujillo realized how vital the development of that trade is for our country, and he has devoted to its enhancement a considerable portion of his thought and action. He has been the first Dominican leader to give such a new orientation to our commercial activity; the first to understand that geographical proximity indicates, over and above all other political considerations, the mutual convenience of commercial exchange, and, as a logic result, the need for closer social, cultural and spiritual ties.

To the advantageous geographical position of our island, to the well-known fertility of its land, and to the short distance that separates it from those natural markets for our goods, President Trujillo has added the weight of some of his most fruitful endeavors — the extensive, modern network of highways and bridges that make inland communications easy; the Trujillo-Hull treaty that restored to the Republic its autonomy in the enactment of customs legislation without foreign interference; the splendid chain of modern hotels in our country's leading cities, and the construction of others to accomodate travelers with the fullest comfort; the new large-capacity Industrial Slaughterhouse and its modern refrigeration plant which supplied meats and meat products to many lands in the West Indies during the war as well as during the rapid growth of that trade in post-war years; the efficient handling and packing of our export products; our incipient merchant marine which, up until the Republic's entry into the last war and despite the sinking of its best ships by German submarines gave and continues to give valuable assistance to our export trade in the West Indies, to which merchant marine he has subsequently added new vessels; the magnificent ports built at Ciudad Trujillo, San Pedro de Macorís, Puerto Plata and Barahona by Benitez Rexach, where even the largest vessels can dock, thanks to Trujillo's unparalleled efforts which fulfilled the dreams of all earlier administrations, and will be unsurpassed in contributing to our commercial and industrial development; and the excellent agricultural policies of his administration which have transformed our country, within a period of a few years, from an importing country into an exporter of many commercial and industrial items, such as rice, lard, butter, vegetable oils, beer, and furniture. He achieved all this while opening wide the country's gates, with thoroughgoing hospiality, to all political refugees, particularly European Jews, whom totalitarian cruelty scattered abroad. In addition, he has taken many other measures that have placed our land on a splendid footing, so that it will become a leading factor in the development of the Caribbean's commercial wealth.

President Trujillo has always maintained that for continental solidarity to become a lasting reality it must be based not only upon the vague though high-sounding ideals of democratic brotherhood but also upon positive commercial advantages reciprocally enjoyed as well as on reciprocal measures for the common defense. In this sense the flag again will follow the dollar, but this time one can hope that it will be the flag of a common ideal that will be unfurled over America.

The policies adopted by President Trujillo for increased trade in the West Indies are a logical central nucleus for his Pan American policies.

The islands of the Caribbean—Puerto Rico, the French and the Dutch West Indies and the Virgin Islands —whose population totals many millions, can become virtually the exclusive consumers of many of our surpluses, particularly in food products, and we, in turn, can become much larger consumers of their industrial products. As may be readily seen, such a trade actually is potentially of far greater importance for the future than for the present, since it lends itself to very considerable expansion once world stability is assured by long term treaties or treaties of indefinite duration that would justify the investment of large sums of domestic and foreign capital in the development of our growing agricultural and livestock industries.

President Trujillo has encountered a great many difficulties in trying to carry out his plans for the expansion of that trade, difficulties that have been due in the main to the mistaken concept of the protectionist policies of the grat powers concerned and to the selfish, uncompromising discriminatory nature of their tariffs. A greater field for our commerce in those and other of the islands of the West Indies as well as parity of our sugar on the United States market with that from other sources in this region, despite furious and frenzied opposition by Cuba, has been and will continue to be one of the principal goals pursued by his administration's diplomacy in the economic field. The unfavorable and unprotected position in which our sugar and other Dominican products have struggled on the world market should have ended with the war. The rule of equal justice for all has always been our standard, and the only way to bring it about permanently is by commercial treaties embodying regional or continent-wide tariff equality and ending once for all every unjust and hateful privilege.

It cannot be gainsaid that for some time now United States commercial policy has been trying to bring about a reduction of customs tariffs that might stimulate a greater exchange of the world's goods. This has been quite evident in recent international meetings held for such a purpose. President Truman has recommended to the Congress that Latin America be given economic assistance. Other influential men in his country have warned of the serious risks involved in withdrawing support from countries which are politically, economically and geographically the real allies nature has provided the United States. The generous attempt envisioned in the Point Four Program, albeit of a limited scope, already has been made the object of diplomatic negotiations with Brazil, Chile, Panama, the Dominican Republic and other nations on this continent. God grant that this sound trend be reaffirmed as a permanent policy of the United States before the urgent present crisis is over, lest its shining promise be forgotten or the enthusiasm of its generous initiators slacken. One should not lose sight of United States practicality; though quite plausible, the trend so far has been naught but a good intention or inclination, nothing really worthwhile having been accomplished yet.

The Dominican Republic's case is a good example. Our sugar, which constitutes our leading industry, is the only sugar that is not protected on the American market. Yet, our import statistics show the United States leading with seventy-five percent of the total, while the total it imports from our country is a mere twenty-eight percent of our shipments abroad. Is this fair? Why, in order to uphold an absurd privilege, refuse us something that would not cause the United States any loss or harm but would bring us prosperity and wellbeing?

Of course, we are speaking of the present situation, and without having lost our hopes that so unfair and unwise a preference will disappear through a more reasonable analysis of our position.

Thanks to President Trujillo's perseverance this fight has not yet been lost. And inasmuch as the cause he defends is a just one and the reasons he invokes are valid we are confident that, Cuba's selfish intransigence notwithstanding, the United States will, in all fairness and reason, satisfy our rightful aspirations.

We must confidently bide the time when those great rectifications will be made. Therefore, in view of the present trend, it cannot be doubted that President Trujillo's trade policies in this area — West Indies trade primarily for the countries of the West Indies — will some day become an accomplished fact. The principles of cooperation and good neighborliness embodied in the doctrine of Pan Americanism which he advoctes will contribute toward achieving the aims of America's great men, bringing to life through his policy for commercial reciprocity throughout this region Bolivar's dream of forming a Union of American States, and Hostos' vision of a West Indies Confederation.

Hostos and Bolívar! Two visionary geniuses whose utopian dreams will thus become tangible reality, thanks to President Trujillo's enlightened actions, for Trujillo is imbued as they were with the highest ideals for our continent, and he is endowed concomitantly with something that was entirely lacking in Bolívar as well as Hostos and that very few persons possess — a deep sense of the practical to inform his actions.

CHAPTER XVIII

AT THE CROSSROADS

A thorough study of the foreign policy of the United States leads one to the conclusion that it has been primarily defensive. During the early period immediately after the United States won its independence, when that country's military might was negligible compared with that of the great nations that shared among themselves dominion over the world, its foreign policy was marked by a set purpose to maintain aloof from any European conflict.

Subsequently, when it had already grown in power, in the face of a probable aggression by the imperialist nations of Europe that formed, at Russia's suggestion and through her endeavors, the so-called Holy Alliance for the deliberate purpose of reconquering and then distributing among themselves Spain's former colonies in the New World and, at the same time, of destroying at the very outset the democratic and republican ideals that those former colonies had adopted in their form of government, the United States proclaimed to the world, with behind-the-scenes support from Great Britain, its famous Monroe Doctrine, couched in strong, challenging terms.

Although that Doctrine was enunciated for the purpose of protecting the self determination of the new-born

Latin American States and to consolidate and reaffirm their freedom, one must agree ,however, that its original concept and its long-range effects were primarily intended by the United States to defend itself and to safeguard its own democratic institutions. The other nations of this continent, therefore, were borne in mind at the time that Doctrine was drafted, not solely because of the sacred principles embodied in the cause they represented, although unquestionably this proved to be a rather important factor, but, above all else, for selfish reasons or strategic and geographic considerations. In other words, the dominant and basic concern in the minds of the great American statesmen who conceived and proclaimed the Monroe Doctrine was, of course, the security and stability of the United States itself. That selfish and purely defensive Doctrine is nevertheless in keeping with the profoundly peaceful sentiments of the American people who, in order to abandon their orderly and industrious life for the purpose of taking up arms, have always required some national catastrophe such as the blowing up of the "Maine", the sinking of the "Lusitania", the treacherous attack upon Pearl Harbor, or the incalculable Korean disaster.

Had it been applied by the United States uniformly and consistently in the sense in which it was originally conceived, the Monroe Doctrine proclaiming the defense of principles that were very noble and very just, although of a selfish nature, could and should have been adopted by all the countries of this hemisphere as their own policy. It is essentially a continental Doctrine.

If that policy had been understood thus from the outset —with its real meaning and its true applicability— instead of producing fears and arousing suspicion among the other nations of this continent, it would have been embraced with sincere enthusiasm. This is so because to defend oneself is human, and we are all willing to admit and quick to understand anything that is human. Viewed within the defensive framework in which it was formulated, the Monroe Doctrine in itself should not have been the cause of the mistrust and fears it has aroused for many decades throughout Latin America.

It has been the abuse of the Doctrine and its arbitrary interpretation bringing about or serving as a pretext for the unwarranted interventions that were carried out in its name, as well as the lack of a more altruistic and broader spirit of understanding on the part of the United States, that always provoked resentment and mistrust. For under the motto of "America for the Americans" and in a clime that was undeniably imperialistic and expansionist there were not wanting events —fortunately now forgotten— that contributed greatly to increasing and, what is worse, to justifying those fears and unfriendly feelings. It was those expedient and versatile interpretations by some of the great statesmen of the United States —interpretations that often were as fully arbitrary as they were shortsighted— that after several decades turned the famous Monroe Doctrine into a positive menace to the security and independence of the weaker nations of this continent rather than a symbol for the defense and protection of all American States.

The Good Neighbor Policy, which has been the noblest and soundest interpretation in American history of the Monroe Doctrine, proved conclusively that neither pressure, subjugation nor violence were necessary for the United States to acquire the use of those ports, bays and airdromes which it might require for either its own defense or for commercial expansion in certain strategic parts of our continent. Friendly pleading and suasion with countries geographically linked for purposes of common defense and the pursuit of common interests proved more availing than the mightiest task force.

A conspicuous example in this connection was set by the Dominican Republic when, under President Trujillo's inspired leadership, it responded with a magnificent, bold gesture to a plea that had been made invoking hemispheric solidarity by offering, at the Pan American Conference in Havana, its manpower, its territory, its airways and its waters for the common defense.

Those were trying times. The victories of the Nazis on the battlefields of Europe were overwhelming and their onward advance seemed irresistible, notwithstanding geographical distances, the threat to the peoples of America and their democratic institutions was a very positive and clear one.

Trujillo did not hesitate a single moment. Realizing that America would find its strength only through unity, he personally cabled precise, forceful instructions to the head of his Government's delegation to that Conference, placing the Dominican Republic's aid unequivocally and resolutely on the side of the great American democracy.

By a strange historical coincidence, it was a President bearing the name of Roosevelt who, by wielding the unburdensome olive branch of his Good Neighbor Policy, abolished, possibly forever, the fear and mistrust that another President Roosevelt had sown through the crushing power of the "Big Stick."

The painful past is not referred to here in order to reopen wounds that the passing of time and a greater rapport have healed, but merely to express the hope cherished by the nations of Latin America in the face of the present new menace, in the sense that true inter-American solidarity will not suffer from arbitrary, tardy or mistaken interpretations.

Russia, the country that led the Holy Alliance in the early part of the nineteenth century, happens to be the one which is now extending its powerful tentacles toward the nations of this continent, while threatening the free and autonomous existence of democratic institutions througout the world.

The main difference between Russian imperialism in the nineteenth century and contemporary Russian imperialism lies in its changed name. Today it is called Communism. However, it has done more than change its name. The weapons and tactics it employs are likewise different and constitute a far greater threat than all the ships and armies that the Holy Alliance could have commanded. Through its subtle, persistent and lying propaganda, which does not unfurl banners on the battlefields but, instead, hides itself and infiltrates surreptitiously wherever there is want or unrest, we now find the enemy within our walls.

Communist infiltration in several American countries, so often denounced publicly by President Trujillo, is clearly evident. Guatemala, Cuba, Venezuela, Chile and Mexico are suffering the results of that infiltration. Its supporters in Guatemala hold public office, Communism's strong influence in the Guatemalan Government has been more than proven. But it is not a "spiritual communism or socialism" such as that of which President Arévalo currently boasts since the United States has taken warning and shown alarm at the growing peril for the free world in Soviet machinations, but authentic Communism that takes direct orders and money from Moscow, as may be seen from the following letter:

CONFIDENTIAL

THE PRESIDENT
OF THE
REPUBLIC OF GUATEMALA
CENTRAL AMERICA

No.:
Ref.: Confidential
In replying, please cite the number and reference of this note.

Mr. Basili Pyakubovsky
Chargé d'Affaires of the USSR.
México, D. F.

Excellency:

The bearer of this letter will place in Your Excellency's hands the most accurate report I am thus far able to submit regarding political and social conditions in Guatemala.

I can assure Your Excellency that up to now everything is in good shape and that, with the wise counsel of your emissaries, the unification of industrial and farm workers of this small country has been achieved.

The Congress, made up almost entirely of elements favorable to myself, will soon delve into all the social problems. Capitalism is afraid but hopes that my administration will bend in its favor.

Your Excellency should not be concerned over the attitude of the former Revolutionary Junta's members, for they are young people lacking in experience and, at any rate, I can eliminate them whenever circumstances may require.

I promise Your Excellency to appoint your friend Luis Cardoza y Aragón as my representative in Moscow so that he may bring about further harmony in the relations between our governments, and Jorge García Granados as Ambassador in Washington, who undoubtedly will render us effective aid.

I wish to express once more my appreciation for Your Excellency's spiritual and financial help, which has enabled us to achieve promptly the consolidation of the working classes.

With my best wishes for Your Excellency's personal health and wellbeing, I am your loyal and good friend.

(signed) Juan José Arévalo

Guatemala, March 18, 1945.

(Seal)

In Cuba, persons of this ilk have held and currently hold high government positions. The United States itself has been victimized by them, both internally and externally. For many years, we have been made the victims of their subversive maneuvering and evil propaganda.

But this time, it is only fair to state, it has not taken another Pearl Harbor to arouse the United States. The resolution which they sponsored and was adopted at Bogotá, immediately after the most violent Communist outbreak ever witnessed in our hemisphere, proves this to be so, though it constitutes only a beginning. But the resolution adopted at that meeting as well as those of other conferences are only so many words devoid of any effect unless they are backed up by responsible action showing a firm, inflexible decision to carry out what has been agreed. Merely reinforcing the almost forgotten Good Neighbor Policy no longer would suffice to prepare our hemisphere to defend itself against an enemy who has fifth columns everywhere. Other means and other methods will have to be brought into play.

This is so because something else is needed besides arms with which to counteract the Russian bombs which may come our way. In this period of a cold war and even open warfare which Communism wages against our institutions, the essential thing would be to intensify and coordinate those measures for the common defense and economic cooperation that are essential for fighting the enemy within our gates.

To ward it off it is necessary to raise the economic level of those backward regions that are still far from achieving a worthwhile industrial development.

Aware of this, President Truman has sponsored, albeit tentatively, certain measures for economic cooperation in favor of some Latin American countries (Brazil, Chile and Argentina); but up to now the accomplisments have been so faint and limited in scope that they fall far short of filling the bill.

It appears, moreover, that the means chosen in these cases —the granting of small loans— despite its beneficial influence for stepping up native industries, is not the only nor even the best manner in which the United States can lend economic cooperation to its friends in our hemisphere.

The United States has the remedy at hand, however. Why not remove the import duties on copper from Chile if the United States needs that mineral for its industrial production? Why should any friendly country's economy be hampered instead of aided? Why does meat from Argentina encounter discriminatory measures that curtail almost completely its importation into the United States? Why does Washington insist upon maintaining the obnoxious privilege of sugar quotas that one country alone in all this hemisphere wants and that spell such great harm for the economic development of another friendly nation? Economic cooperation and technical assistance, equal treatment and credit facilities, are the things we need, and they are what the United States can give to the other American republics. Political, economic and military leadership implies grave responsibility alongside of great advantages. World supremacy has a price. In wartime, it is paid in blood. In peace time, with economic and moral responsibility.

Communism can be defeated at its source. Its own principal means of attack are economic. The main defense against it must therefore be through economic means. Wherever there is want, unemployment and unrest the answer must be peace, work and social justice.

The answer to contemporary Russia must be fully as resolute, firm and forceful an answer as that which was given to Czarist Russia through the Monroe Doctrine against the Holy Alliance. But this time the answer must be underscored with deeds such as those the United States has accomplished in Greece and Turkey. Our hemisphere needs a Marshall Plan for the Americas. A united, prosperous continent sharing common goals and ideas, wherein nations help and respect one another, will be an insurmountable barrier to communism.

America is once again at the crossroads, and any vacillation may prove fatal.

Preparedness must not wait for another Pearl Harbor unleashed by the Russians. The wise and practical thing is to prepare now, for tomorrow will be too late.

II

It seems idle to talk of peace at a time when the world faces once more the horror of another World War. Still, the catastrophe for Christian civilization we are facing would involve such dire consequences that many persons refuse to believe that the world has lost its mind or that a peace based on justice, freedom and the emancipating principles of social justice can no longer be secured.

Each time that one ponders the horrors of war and the annihilation of one people by another, the more convinced one becomes of the need to end once for all this terrible scourge of mankind.

But, how can this be achieved? Through the centuries men have tried different formulas for avoiding wars such as alliances, the balance of power, isolation, arbitration treaties, non-aggression pacts, and the League of Nations.

Two thousand years ago, Christ preached his doctrine of Justice and Peace among men, so that instead of hating they should love one another. Over six hundred years ago, Pierre Dubois proposed for the first time an international court for arbitration. Over a century ago Bolivar planned his Federation of American Nations. Several decades have gone by since Woodrow Wilson created the League of Nations for the preservation of democracy and the prevention of wars. Fifteen years ago President Trujillo submitted his plan to create a League of American Nations, reviving the magnanimous Liberator's dream to save the Americas from all aggression and to preserve their independence, which project has become, after several subterfuges and delays, a promising reality in the shape of the inter-American body known as the Organization of American States. Despite the discouraging failure of the League of Nations, Wilson's ideal of a world organization for peace and security, adopted by Roosevelt, Churchill and Stalin during World War II, in time became the powerful group that we know as the United Nations. When one speaks nowadays of a United States of Europe people no longer smile disdainfully as though it were an impossible Utopia, as they did when French Premier Briand proposed it; they now view it as a probable future reality.

But, will those organizations prove to be really, positively and definitely efficient? Won't selfishness, ambition, covert hypocrisy and dissimilar political tendencies divide these nations and leave them shorn of strength, cohesion and unity?

Notwithstanding the constant and timely warnings given by the Dominican Government, the Organization of American States was unable to prevent that the dangerous situation created in the Caribbean since 1947, with the avowed complicity of the Cuban Government under President Grau San Martín first and later under President Prío Socarrás, and of the Government of Guatemala under the passionate communist Arévalo as well as the Venezuelan Government under the two communistic Rómulos (Betancourt and Gallegos) should become a positive and genuine threat against the peace and security of America. It was unable to prevent the attempted invasion from Cayo Confites, a Cuban island that the revolutionists chose as their springboard, that constituted an aggression carried out with loud proclamations and employing Cuban Government funds, trucks, ships and personnel in flagrant violation of the existing inter-American pacts for non-intervention. (1) Nor was it able to prevent the invasion of the Dominican Republic along the shores of Luperón, which was organized and led by officials of the Guatemalan and Cuban governments and wherein unwary youths of various nationalities who had been seduced by the siren strains of hidden subversive elements met their death or were taken prisoner. Those hostile activities, which were real acts of war, were carried out despite repeated warnings which the Dominican Government gave to all and sundry and official communications it addressed to the aforementioned

(1) See **Appendix IV.**

Governments as well as to the appropriate inter-American organs concerning the constant revolutionary activity of the so-called Caribbean Legion.

On the other hand, the United Nations, having made an armed stand against Communist aggression on the Korean peninsula, has had its troops suffer all manner of hardships and even defeat in the early days of that conflict. At a time when, if anything, there should be greater unity among the nations that ought to contribute to the fullest of their ability and in adequate proportion to the common effort, bitter and discouraging mutual criticisms are heard.

However, we should not be altogether pessimistic. The action by the United Nations up to now is beyond any just complaints. It is a fact that, due to the steadfast efforts of great statesmen and the firmness which the United States has shown on this occasion, all hopes for a peaceful and honorable settlement of the issues at stake through negotiation have not been lost, in a final and supreme effort to prevent catastrophe and end the unspeakable anguish that now oppresses mankind, and, failing this, for the imposition of punitive sanctions against the aggressors.

Present day wars are all the more cruel because the effects of warfare have become more widespread as man has increased his scientific and technological knowledge and become more civilized. Scientific progress has been applied more for destruction than otherwise. New destructive weapons, weapons of hate and vengeance, atomic bombs and flying rockets, pilotless planes and lethal gases of shocking violence have been added to the arsenal of destructive methods. Each passing day will bring some new invention for destruction and if another World War should befall us it is certain that there will not be a single nation on earth exempt from its deadly effects, be it large or small. The oceans will become as small lakes; the highest and steepest mountains will be within arm's reach, and the greatest depths of the earth, its most heavily protected caves, as well as its most guarded shelters, will be readily accesible to asphyxiating gases and germ warfare.

In centuries past mercenary armies of any nationality would defend, in distant lands, the banner of some monarch who was not their own king. Subsequently, during the Napoleonic era, powerful national armies, scientifically trained to kill, would decide in a few pitched battles the fate of a republic or an empire. In 1914 and 1939 whole nations fighting one another with unprecedented fury on land and in the air, on the seas as well as beneath their waters — wherever there might be lives to snuff out or accumulated wealth to destroy— reached the highest pitch of madness, for it was not merely a question of battles between armies but of fierce, relentless combat between one population and another.

Of course, mankind cannot continue this ad infinitum, with a new World War every few years. Under the threat of immediate or imminent war, its faith in the effectiveness of civilization would disappear, its love of initiative and even of life itself would lose, through such a repetition, its strongest stimulus and its great force.

In the United Nations an attempt has been made to correct the principal cause for the failure of the League of Nations —the absence of any potential force to impose its sanctions and support its decisions. This was proved by prompt action in the case of aggression against Korea. There still remains, however, the unequal representation of sovereignty through the monopoly exercised by the five great powers who control the Security Council and through the veto power which the Soviet Union has so grossly abused.

We cannot lose sight of what happened to the League of Nations.

When the totalitarian states regarded circumstances as being propitious and felt that the time was ripe to succeed in their ambitious and evil purposes, they loosed their waves of aggression upon the world, first tentatively and later with unlimited and overwhelming force. And the League of Nations that President Wilson founded was unable to resist their savage onslaught.

The first blow was in China. The Japanese invaded Manchuria. What should the League have done? In keeping with its duty, it should have pounced upon Japan and controlled it. But it hesitated, cowered, and failed to do so. The efforts made by Mr. Stimpson, the then Secretary of State of the United States, a non-member country, proved unavailing. Britain, looking after its own interests, turned a deaf ear, and Mr. Stimson contented himself with non-recognition of those territories acquired through conquest. Selfishness prevailed.

After all, thinking things through carefully, what did a Britisher in Manchester, a Dane in Copenhaguen or a Norwegian in Oslo, although their countries were members of the League, care for what might happen to a Chinaman in Manchuria? They failed to see in Manchuria's fate any peril, either immediate or remote, for their commercial or individual interests or for their own nation. Who wanted to go to war over something as far away as China? The second attack was in Africa. Italy invaded Abyssinia. And what did the League of Nations do besides invoking fulfillment of the Pact? Nothing. It did not even dare deprive Italy of the gasoline which it needed for the tanks and airplanes of its invading armies. Britain made timid attempts to stop Italy, but this time it was the Americans' turn to pay no attention and to heed only their own interests, evening their score with Britain. After bluffing the British, those masters of bluffing, Mussolini got his way and swallowed up Abyssinia. Thinking things through carefully, what did a region in Africa matter to a Dutchman in The Hague, to a Uraguayan in Montevideo or to a millionaire in New York? Who would have dared suggest going to war so that the Abyssinians might remain independent? It is true that it meant sacrificing a nation that was a League member. It is likewise true that thereby the freedom of a people was jeopardized and the freedom of all was indirectly threatened. But the counsels of selfishness weighed far more in the scales than those of common reason, and the sacrifice was consummated. Then came Austria, Czechoslovakia, Poland, Pearl Harbor and Singapore. It took a long time to overcome selfishness and to shake the democracies from their complacent inertia, from their mental Maginot line. This is why they had to fight one country after another, for the same reasons for which, with greater foresight and determined spirit, they should have fought from the begining and avoided the sacrifice of millions of lives and untold suffering for mankind.

The menace of totalitarian Fascism passed. But now mankind is faced with an even greater peril, Communism, which is like a terrible monster out of a nightmare. Will the United Nations be able to hold back this avalanche? Will they be prepared, unified and willing to accomplish this tremendous effort at the right time? Let us hope so, although this time the selfishness of the great powers has already reared its head more than once, as with the former League of Nations. The same vacillation now paralyzes its action. When the moment comes for paramount decisions, they are averted through skilfull compromise, sometimes because of occult defeatism. Meanwhile Communism advances more and more, infiltrating wherever there is unrest or want or where injustice reigns. It is a hushed, surreptitious advance, in silent waves such as those beating against the shores of Latin America or in a furious onslaught with resounding explosions such as in Indo-China, Malaya and the Republic of Korea. All this notwithstanding, selfishness may continue to be rampant. Anti-Communist Spain is still snubbed, or if it does get any help at all it is grudgingly granted, in so slow, minuscule and contemptuous a manner that it may well be resented more than appreciated. And despite its open and implacable enmity for Soviet Russia, Yugoslavia is allowed to almost perish from hunger.

We are living a dark night of uncertainty. Will there be found eventually, amid the engulfing chaos about us, a light, some bright spot that will guide us on our march ahead? Will peaceful methods lead us, through a conciliation of so many opposing interests, to the desired stage of agreement, the coveted goal of freedom and justice that will halt the obdurate in their tracks, open their eyes to the truths of Christianity and give to men the peace and the bread they so direly need? Or is it that mankind's travail is to be without end?

That is an inscrutable enigma of the future that in these times of terrible confusion, anguish and despair no one but God can solve.

PART FOUR

TRUJILLO'S ADMINISTRATION

CHAPTER XIX

PAST AND PRESENT
RELEVANCE OF FACTS AND FIGURES

POPULATION CENSUS OF THE DOMINICAN REPUBLIC

In 1935 the total population of the Dominican Republic was 1,479,417; the figure for the male population was 750,704, while that for the female population was 728,713. In 1950, our total population is 2,121,083; of this total, 1,063,759 are male and 1,057,324 female. Ciudad Trujillo, capital of the Republic, has 181,533 inhabitants of whom 84,103 are male and 97,430 female. In 1935 the population of Ciudad Trujillo was 116,992.

I

DEPARTMENT OF WAR, NAVY AND AVIATION

This Department has, in addition to its titular functions, responsibility for the following services: Port Authority, Lighthouses, Pilots and Coast Guard, Selective Service, and the Government's Merchant Marine. The Military Institute of Geography, the Weather Bureau and the Maritime and Aeronautical Commissions are also under its jurisdiction.

The National Army is constantly progressing with regard to equipment and supplies as well as the technical training required in order to maintain itself at the enviable peak of efficiency to which President Trujillo has raised it.

The devotion of the Army to its distinguished Commander-in-Chief and the deep sense of duty with which each and every one of its members is imbued were demonstrated by the heroic deed performed by Private Leopoldo

Puente Rodríguez who single-handedly and on his own initiative attacked the group of invaders who landed at Luperón.

The Medical Corps of the National Army has a select body of physicians, dentists and specialists, graduates of our University, who perform their duties with real enthusiasm, devotion and efficiency. Besides the excellent and praiseworthy "Profesor Marión" Military Hospital, which was donated to the Army by Generalissimo Trujillo, there are many medical and dental dispensaries throughout the country, each under the supervision of a graduate medical or dental officer.

The Army has two Training Centers where the soldiers are taught modern techniques by a staff of officers of proven competence.

At the Army Arsenal in San Cristóbal weapons are manufactured and repaired. Today, the Republic no longer needs to import infantry weapons. The Army itself manufactures them.

Selective Service carries on its rolls the names of 467,704 citizens who freely volunteered to register. Of these, 57,068 have been given a seventeen weeks' course in basic military training.

Navy

The National Navy was non-existent prior to 1930. The warships purchased by President Heureaux disappeared. Today, thanks to President Trujillo's tireless efforts, our Navy possesses sufficient units to meet our need for a constant patrol of our shores. This was demonstrated in the rapid and decisive action taken by Coast Patrol Vessel No. 9 on the night of June 19, 1949 off the coast of Luperón, against the Catalina flying boat that carried a group of insurgents of the so-called Caribbean Legion. In a matter of seconds the aircraft was destroyed.

The Naval Academy, whose staff includes Dominicans as well as foreigners, is further proof of President Trujillo's wholehearted desire to train our Armed Forces with scientific efficiency. The thorough and meticulous training, gentlemanly conduct and ever higher standards of the officers and men of our National Navy are a source of real pride to our country.

Following the cruel blow inflicted on our shipping by German submarines which sank our two best ships, the steamships **San Rafael** and **Presidente Trujillo** on May 3, 1941 and May 21, 1941, respectively, it appeared that, except for a few schooners and skiffs, our Merchant Marine had ceased to exist. For some time now, President Trujillo has been engaged in promoting our Merchant Marine. To that end, the Government purchased the 3,501 ton steamship **Nuevo Dominicano**, the tanker **24 de Octubre** and the **Ciudad Trujillo.** The **Nuevo Dominicano** is a beautiful passenger and cargo vessel that plies the Ciudad Trujillo, Kingston, Miami and Nassau route and has all the comforts to be found in a ship of its class. In order to cope with whatever problem might arise relative to the development of our Merchant Marine, President Trujillo has established a Maritime Commission.

Military Aviation

Our air corps is a model of efficiency. The number of aircraft and the skill of its pilots and mechanics place it among the first in the West Indies.

As in the case of the other branches of our Armed Forces, President Trujillo has given priority to our Military aviation which is entirely a creation of his inasmuch as before 1930 it was non-existent. Its carefully selected officer corps receives practical and theoretical instruction at the Military Aviation School where competent Dominican and foreign instructors teach the most advanced techniques. Furthermore, President Trujillo has sent many officers to several schools in the United States and other countries where they have received specialized training in the diverse aspects of aviation, especially in radio communications and in the servicing, repair and maintenance of aircraft.

Civil Aviation

As a natural result of the astounding progress achieved by our military aviation, our civil aviation has been intensively developed. The Compañía Dominicana de Aviación, Inc., which owns several large high-speed airplanes, not only has daily scheduled service between several cities of the Republic but has extended its operations to certain countries in the Caribbean and South America. President Trujillo has established an Aeronautics Commission as an agency of the Department of War, Navy and Aviation in order to study and solve problems relative to the development of our civil aviation.

Military Schools

Future officers and non-commissioned specialists receive remarkably efficient training in the National Army schools such as those for Cadets, Radio-Telegraphy and Signal Communications, and the Riding Academy. The latter has added to its training program the game of polo which, besides being interesting and enjoyable, serves to further develop horsemanship.

Office of the Quartermaster General of the Armed Forces

The Office of the Quartermaster General of the Armed Forces, as indicated by its title, is responsible for administration. Under this Office are included: the Textile Shop, responsible for the manufacture of first and second class materiel; the Folding Cot Shop, in charge of the manufacture and repair of that equipment; the Print Shop, responsible for all the printing work of the Armed Forces; the Typewriter Repair Shop, which completed 913 repair jobs during 1950; and the Machine Shop, which is responsible for all mechanical repairs on vehicles of the Armed Forces. Under the Office of the Quartermaster General and subject to its Regulations there are also quartermaster offices within each branch of the Armed Forces, which render to the respective branches the same services performed by the Office of the Quartermaster General for the Armed Forces as a whole.

Military Institute of Geography

Law No. 2136 of October 22, 1949 established the Military Institute of Geography as a unit of the Department of War, Navy and Aviation under the supervision of the Office of the Chief of Staff of the Army. The former National Council on Geography and Cartography of the Department of the Interior and Police and the Institute of Geography and Geology of the University of Santo Domingo were combined to form the Military Institute of Geography. It initiated its work on January 1, 1950, having as its specific duties the coordination and supervision of all cartographic, geodetic and photogrammetric work, as well as research relative to the boundaries of the Republic.

Artillery Battalion

The Artillery Battalion comprises all the heavy weapons of the Army. Its headquarters is on kilometer 4½ of Sánchez Highway. It possesses all the arms necessary to its mission and its officers are well trained; some received training abroad, while others were trained in the Dominican Republic by foreign technicians.

Cavalry Squadron

The Cavalry Squadron is comprised of the mounted troops of the Army and is correspondingly equipped. Some of the mounts are of the imported "Morgan" breed, while others are of native breed. Its headquarters is located at kilometer 7½ of Duarte Highway.

II

DEPARTMENT OF THE INTERIOR, POLICE AND COMMUNICATIONS

This Department is responsible for matters relative to the provinces and municipalities. Under the Department are included: the National Police, the General Office of Immigration, the National Archives, and the Commission for Public Entertainment and Radio.

In 1930 there were only 12 provinces in the Republic. President Trujillo created new provinces in order to "Dominicanize" the frontier areas and to distribute more equitably throughout the national territory the beneficial activities of the government. At present there are 20 provinces, and the District of Santo Domingo. There is a Governor of the District of Santo Domingo in addition to the 20 Provincial Governors. Each of the latter represents the Executive Power within the limits of his jurisdiction, acting from the capital of the province, assuring compliance with the laws and regulations and reporting to the President through the appropriate cabinet officer. The Governors are appointed by the President of the Republic. Each township has its own government consisting of the President of the Town Council and aldermen, elected to office by popular vote. Vacancies are filled as provided by law. Each township is subdivided into wards headed by one or more ward leaders appointed by the Council.

Prior to 1930 only 21 cities had electric light and power, and with the exception of the most important cities such service was very deficient. By 1950, this essential service had been extended to a total of 78 cities and communities.

Prior to 1930 only 3 cities possessed aqueducts and lesser water systems. In 1950, a total of 49 aqueducts are distributed among all the important cities. There are 183 lesser water supply systems scattered throughout the rural communities. In the era of Trujillo we find a total of 225 communities enjoying this important service.

National Police

The National Police was created by President Trujillo by virtue of an Executive Decree of March 2, 1936. He thereby integrated into a single police force the separate municipal police bodies which existed prior to that date. The present authorized strength of the National Police is as follows:

1 Colonel, Chief of the National Police
2 Lieutenant Colonels
1 Major, Legal Consultant
3 Majors
15 Captains
1 First Lieutenant, Technician
25 First Lieutenants
31 Second Lieutenants
9 Sergeant Majors

14 Sergeants, Administration and Accounting
67 Sergeants
116 Corporals
1.160 Privates

Total 1.545 Officers and men

The importance and usefulness of the services rendered by the National Police are evident from the fact that it comprises:

A) A General Headquarters directly under the orders of the Chief of the National Police. It deals with all matters referred by the departments and units of the Force such as enlistments, separations, transfers, recommendations for promotion, recommendations for appointments and dismissals. All correspondence addressed to higher headquarters and to other Departments of the Government is cleared through it. It deals with all matters pertaining to the proper functioning of the National Police.

B) An Identification and Registration Office under the Major who is the Legal Consultant. This Office maintains a Register of all foreign residents through personal identification cards; of all the personnel of the National Police; all chauffeurs and operators of motor vehicles; daily reports of transients in hotels, boarding and rooming houses; a Register of servants and domestic workers; and reports of the whereabouts of badges and weapons of the members of the National Police.

C) A Secret Service Department, headed by a Major of the National Police. This department renders services of the utmost importance.

D) The Legal Consultant's Office. This Office deals with legal points at issue that may arise in the Force and represents it in juridical matters. Furthermore, it consults with other agencies on the files of members of the National Police.

E) A Robbery Investigation Division, under a Captain. This Department receives complaints and carefully investigates robberies, attempted robberies and damages, and initiates the appropriate procedures for persecution.

F) A Highway Police Department headed by a Captain who is responsible for the enforcement of Law No. 2556 governing vehicle traffic.

G) A Traffic Company, headed by a Captain. This unit is responsible for facilitating vehicle and pedestrian traffic in the nation's capital and in the larger cities.

H) A General Quartermaster's Office, under a Captain. This Office provides all supplies required by the National Police in order to carry out its duties.

I) Members of the National Police especially designated by the Chief represent the Force in the courts.

J) The National Police has its own machine shop which is under the supervision of a First Lieutenant, Technician. This shop is responsible for the maintenance and repair of the vehicles of the Force.

K) The National Police has its own publication, **La Revista de Policía** ("The Police Review") which is published quarterly. This publication is edited and published by the Legal Consultant.

L) The National Police has a modern radiocommunications system with transmitting stations in the headquarters building.

M) The National Police has a band, that of the Administrative Council of the District of Santo Domingo, under the direction of a Captain.

N) There are four Disciplinary Tribunals to examine and pass on charges of grave breaches of discipline: The Central Department Tribunal in Ciudad Trujillo; the Northern Department Tribunal in Santiago de los Caballeros; the Southern Department Tribunal in San Juan de la guana; and the Eastern Department Tribunal in San Pedro de Macorís. A defense attorney is provided for all those accused of grave breaches of discipline.

O) There are four territorial divisions of the National Police: the Central Department, in Ciudad Trujillo; the Northern Department in Santiago de los Caballeros; the Southern Department in San Juan de la Maguana; and the Eastern Department of San Pedro de Macorís. Each is headed by a high ranking officer, and the different Companies of the National Police are subordinate to these Departments.

P) The National Police has modern barber shops available to all its members.

Q) President Trujillo established a Retirement Pension for members of the National Police who, because of physical or mental incapacity or because of advanced age can no longer render service. Members of the service who have served for twenty years are eligible for a pension.

R) The Chief of the National Police makes periodic general inspections to obtain a first-hand picture of conditions and to ensure the proper functioning of the force.

S) In honor of the members of the National Police, President Trujillo has set aside March 2 of each year as "Policeman's Day", thus commemorating the anniversary of the establishment of the force.

A comparison, however brief and succinct, of the old Municipal Police with the present National Police established by Trujillo shows an astounding contrast. Prior to the Era of Trujillo, the former was maintained and directed by the Town Councils; its personnel was poorly paid, clothed and fed and with regard to intelligence quotients as well as moral and social qualifications it was most deficient. The new Force, which comprises select personnel who have undergone rigorous examinations, is well organized, well-trained and properly outfitted. The officers of the National Police Corps are competent and remarkably well manered. They are unyielding in the performance of their duty but courteous in their dealings with the public. The organization of the National Police constitutes another of President Trujillo's great achievments.

General Office of Immigration

This agency is directly under the Secretary of the Interior and Police. Its duties include the issuance of Residence Permits and their renewal, the issuance of Re-entry

Permits to resident foreigners travelling abroad, the repatriation of indigent foreigners, and the deportation of foreigners whenever prescribed by law.

The following data indicate the scope of this agency's activities:

Tax Revenue in 1950

Immigration and Surtax Stamps	DR$205,497.46
Residence Permits	DR$254,394.80
Re-entry Permits	RD$ 17,660.00
Certificates of Exit	DR$ 2,854.00
Personal Identification Cards	DR$ 497.00
Miscellaneous Certificates	DR$ 28.00
Travel Documents for Refugees or Stateless Persons	DR$ 360.00
Administrative Fines	DR$ 490.00

Air Traffic

During 1950, 3,279 airplanes from foreign airports landed at the "General Andrews Airport" at Ciudad Trujillo, representing a monthly average of 273 planes. 20,133 passengers entered the country and 21,277 left by air.

Maritime Traffic

During 1950, 1,659 sailing vessels and steamships arrived at Dominican ports, representing a monthly average of 138 ships.

Other International Traffic

A total of 347 vehicles crossed the border, of which 175 entered the country and 172 left.

General Office of Communications

Income from communications reached a peak in 1950—DR$675,074.49, despite a considerable reduction in air postage rates.

The total number of postal deliveries during 1950 was 19,876,369, a peak in the history of the Communications Service.

In 1930 the total number of Telegraph, Telephone and Post Offices was 82. In 1950 there are 112, of which 23 are first-class offices. Many are located in especially constructed Government buildings. The Palace of Communications in Ciudad Trujillo is a model edifice.

The National Archives

The National Archives, an important center of our cultural history, were established thanks to President Trujillo's unflagging interest in and wholehearted devotion to everything related to our past, which abounds with visissitudes paralleling those in the history of our archives.

Prior to 1935, the National Archives had led a precarious existence, located in inadequate, cramped installations where the documents, books and registers corresponding to the archives of the different governmental departments were stored in complete disorder. Very rarely loving hands rescued some of those priceless documents.

In 1935, on the initiative of President Trujillo, Law 912 was promulgated. This law provided for the scientific and methodical organization of the National Archives and was supplemented by regulations embodied in Decree 1316 of that same year. Subsequently, the original law and the regulations were amended by Law 1085 and Decree 1590-bis, respectively, both of which went into effect in 1936 and are still in force.

A more adequate building, competent personnel and modern equipment were provided. In 1941, thanks to the constant interest of their illustrious founder, the National Archives were lodged in the beautiful building which they now occupy on Arzobispo Nouel Street.

Thus, the National Archives which formerly were simply a depository for old papers were converted into a cultural center at the service of all. Visitors and research workers, both foreign and national, visit it frequently.

In 1943, a short course in classification was given at the National Archives for the benefit of its personnel and of persons interested in the subject.

From 1941 to 1943, representatives of the institution were engaged in work at the National Archives of Cuba in Havana, in accordance with an agreement. The purpose of this mission, in keeping with its instructions, was to undertake reasearch in documents related to the history of Santo Domingo and to copy them. Copies were made, **in extenso,** of 1,958 files and file cards and of 104 documents. Many of the latter were published in the Bulletin of the National Archives.

The Bulletin, which is the publicity medium of the institution, was first published in 1938. Its material has included the texts of many documents copied from the National Archives and foreign sources. Historians and research workers who have specialized in our history are numbered among its contributors. This publication is considered one of the best of its type in America.

In 1944 the institution initiated a series of special publications which have been enthusiastically received by persons specializing in historical studies. This series includes the **Relaciones Históricas de Santo Domingo** ("Historical Relations of Santo Domingo"), Collection and Notes by E. Rodríguez Demorizi, in two volumes; **Documentos para la Historia de la República Dominicana** ("Documents bearing on the History of the Dominican Republic"), Collection of E. Rodríguez Demorizi, in two volumes; **Correspondencia del Cónsul de Francia en Santo Domingo** ("Correspondence of the French Consul in Santo Domingo"), Edition and Notes of E. Rodríguez Demorizi, in two volumes; **Samaná, Pasado y Porvenir,** ("Samaná, Past and Future"); **San Cristóbal de Antaño** ("Old San Cristóbal"); **Manuel Rodríguez Objío** ("Manuel Rodríguez Objío, Poet, Hero of the Restoration, Historian, Martyr", by Ramón Lugo Lovatón; **Relaciones** ("Relations") by Manuel Rodríguez Objío, Introduction, Titles and Notes by Ramón Lugo Lovatón, the **Indice General del Boletín del 1938 al 1944** ("General Index of the Bulletin from 1938 to 1944").

The National Archives has the largest existing collection of national newspapers, both old and new, including the very important collection of the **Listin Diario,** which it purchased, and that of **La Opinión**, which was donated. The newspaper collections are material used most by research workers who go daily to the Research Room of the institution.

The Library of the National Archives consists largely of historical Dominican works whose quality and quantity are indicative of the intensive work being carried out in the field of the culture and history of the Dominican Republic.

Appropriations for the National Archives are constantly increasing. This is but natural inasmuch as it is responsible for the preservation and filing of practically all documents, files, registers and other papers of purely historical interest from the archives of all government departments and agencies, the District of Santo Domingo and other communities.

Among projects whose early initiation is planned by President Trujillo there is included a building for the National Archives and Library. This project will undoubtedly constitute another of his outstanding achievements and will embellish the city which bears his illustrious name.

III

ADMINISTRATIVE DEPARTMENT OF THE EXECUTIVE POWER

This Department is responsible for all correspondence received and dispatched by the President of the Republic. It also keeps him abreast of all information that is useful to the administration and renders all services relative to the Executive Power which are not delegated by legislation to other departments.

The following figures for 1950 give an indication of the work carried out by this Department:

Communications dispatched	42,099
Telephone and Telegraphic Communications	3,473
Appointments to Official Positions Handled	9,090

Additional responsibilities include: the Legal Advisory Office of the Executive Power, the Bureau of the Budget, the Administrative Council of the District of Santo Domingo, and the Coordinating Commission for Direct Purchases.

The Legal Advisory Office advises and reports on the legal aspects of cases submitted to it and also prepares legislation, regulations and decrees. In 1950, it submitted 1,511 reports.

The Bureau of the Budget prepares the budget under the direction of the President and supervises the appropriate application of the Law on Public Expenditures.

IV

DEPARTMENT OF FOREIGN AFFAIRS AND WORSHIP

The international prestige of the Dominican Republic has kept pace with its remarkable moral, material and economic progress so that today it has reached a level never even dreamt of prior to the Trujillo Era.

Because of the irreproachable manner in which the Trujillo administration conducts its internal affairs, the seriousness and punctuality with which it meets its international obligations, and the loftiness of the principles governing the country's relations with other nations, the Dominican Republic, whose very existence was practically ignored by many nations in years gone by, today ranks high among the civilized nations of the world. It has won this prestige through adherence to moral principles, its civic progress and its conscientious dignity that is free from both unbecoming haughtiness and abject servility.

The history of Santo Domingo's diplomatic and consular relations with foreign powers before the Era of Trujillo is quite shameful. This is true not only of our early history as an independent nation, when the Consuls of Spain, France and the United States, acting like veritable Roman Proconsuls, successfully demanded of our country shameful reparations for any real or supposed insult to their nationals and brought to bear their overwhelming influence in the decisions of our Government, as evidenced by the fact that they sometimes participated with the right to express themselves and to vote in the Cabinet's sessions. It is likewise true of more recent years during which a useless and unnecessary servility deprived our diplomacy of even a pretense of autonomy and independence. Undoubtedly, there have been some outstanding exceptions to this rule, such as that of the austere and irreproachable José María Cabral y Báez who, as our Minister of Foreign Affairs, opposed American imperialism in 1916. Nonetheless, generally speaking, our diplomatic history was one of complacent and comfortable subordination of the nation's interests to the prevalent political interests of other countries, often resulting in humiliating and shameful betrayals of patriotic duty.

Nowadays, thanks to the loyal probity of Trujillo and his conciliatory yet dignified policy, the Republic has made great strides, surmounting difficulties, disproving calumnies with facts and blocking the shafts of envy with the shield of its good faith. Trujillo's advent to power marks a radical change in our diplomacy. Now, as never before in our history, the country's honor is defended with dignity at all times and under every circumstance.

Under Trujillo's aegis, Dominican diplomacy has won significant and deserved triumphs. The good name of the Republic has been enhanced by the following glorious achievements of Trujillo: his proposal for a League of American Nations, which embodies his ideas regarding continental solidarity, which was supported by Colombia, and has finally been largely crystalized in the present Organization of American States; his timely endeavors in behalf of peace at the time of the Chaco War between Bolivia and Paraguay; his Treaty with Haiti that delimited the frontier with that country, brilliantly terminating a vexing centuries-old problem; his patriotic policy toward the United States that finally led to the cancellation of the Dominican-United States Convention through the Trujillo-Hull Treaty restoring our financial freedom; his generous offer at Evian in behalf of stateless persons and exiles; his policy of frank, vigorous and unvarnished opposition to imperialistic communism, against which peril he was the first to raise a cry of alarm in America; his resolute and serious policy in the face of the simultaneous attacks of Grau San Martín and the Prío Socarrás clique in Cuba, Rómulo Betancourt and his puppet in Venezuela, as well as Arévalo of Guatemala, that unmitigated muscovite; and his sincere defense in the United Nations of the Government of Generalissimo Franco, the head of the Spanish State, with persevering endeavors in the face of solid and powerful opposition until he achieved his goal of recognition of that government by the most important powers of America and Europe.

The talks held on February 19, 1951 between President Trujillo and President Magloire of Haiti in the border cities of Elías Piña, Dominican Republic, and Belladere, Haiti, established the base for a frank and loyal understanding between both nations, as indicated by the text of the following communiqué which was published on that date:

JOINT DECLARATION

Inspired by a desire to cooperate loyally toward closer and more positive ties in the relations between their respective governments; convinced that, to this end, they should seek to find lasting solutions to the problems that concern both countries in order to achieve, within a spirit of peace and harmony, a united front in view of the extraordinary situation created by the aggressive policy of international communism and to thus contribute, together with countries of the American continent and in particular with the other countries of the Caribbean and of the Gulf of Mexico, to the defense of their political, social and economic security;

His Excellency, the President of the Dominican Republic, Rafael L. Trujillo Molina, and His Excellency, the President of the Republic of Haiti, Paul E. Magloire, met for an important talk on February 19, 1951, which was initiated in the Dominican border city of Elías Piña and continued in the Haitian border city of Belladere.

During the aforesaid talk the Dominican and Haitian heads of State have agreed:

1) To orient the policy of their respective chancelleries toward the speedy conclusion of a bilateral Agreement designed to strengthen the multi-lateral convention concluded in Havana in February, 1928 relative to the

Rights and Duties of States in the event of civil strife and to apply specifically Resolution VI of the II Meeting of Consultation of Ministers of Foreign Affairs of the American Republics;

2) To regulate the migratory movements of Dominican and Haitian nationals in the respective territories of both countries in an adequate manner, in keeping with circumstances, through the adoption of an effective diplomatic instrument;

3) To grant mutual customs concessions in order to develop trade between the two countries; and

4) To proceed to the conclusion of cultural and tourist agreements in order to promote the understanding and friendship that should henceforth characterize relations between the two countries.

Their Excellencies Presidents Trujillo and Magloire have arrived at a general agreement regarding everything relative to the coordinated and joint action of both governments to the end that their cooperation in the political, economic and social fields shall be inspired by the geographic proximity of both countries which share the island's territory and that it shall faithfully reflect the international commitments subscribed to in defense of the principles of justice, freedom and democracy.

Elías Piña, February 19, 1951

Diplomatic Representation

A brief comparison of the number and category of our present diplomatic and consular missions with those in a not too distant past will give a clear idea of the remarkable progress achieved in this field.

In 1930 there was not a single accredited foreign diplomat with the rank of ambassador in the Republic; Haiti, the United States, Cuba, France and Germany had Ministers Plenipotentiary in Ciudad Trujillo. Spain, Venezuela, and the United Kingdom had Chargés d'Affaires.

In 1951 the following nations have ambassadors at Ciudad Trujillo, in addition to the Holy See's Nuncio: Spain, Nicaragua, the United States, Brazil, México, Perú, Argentina, France, Haití, Colombia, Venezuela, and the United Kingdom.

The following nations maintain Ministers Plenipotentiary in Ciudad Trujillo: Italy, Honduras, Panamá, El Salvador, and Ecuador. Chargés d'Affaires are maintained by Paraguay, China, Chile, Cuba and Uruguay. The following nations have Ministers Plenipotentiary and Chargés d'Affaires accredited to our Government but with residence in other countries: Belgium, Czecho-Slovakia, Poland, Denmark, Holland, Sweden and Norway.

In 1950 the Dominican Republic had Ambassadors accredited to the following countries and international organizations: the United Nations, the Organization of American States, the United States of America, Brazil, México, Colombia, Nicaragua, Chile, Venezuela, Perú, the Holy See, France, Spain, Argentina, the United Kingdom and Haiti. It has Ministers Plenipotentiary in Honduras, El Salvador, Panama, Italy and Switzerland. There are resident Chargés d'Affaires in Ecuador, Paraguay, Cuba, Uruguay, Bolivia, Portugal and Holland.

Consular Representation

Career and honorary Consuls General, Consuls and Vice Consuls are maintained in Ciudad Trujillo by Argentina, Belgium, Bolivia, Colombia, Costa Rica, Denmark, Ecuador, Lebanon, El Salvador, Spain, the United States, Finland, the United Kingdom, Greece, Haiti, Chile, Honduras, Nicaragua, Norway, Holland, Panamá, Sweden, Switzerland, Uruguay, and Venezuela.

The Dominican Republic has career Consuls in New York, Miami, New Orleans, San Juan, Ponce and Mayaguez in Puerto Rico, Montreal, Havana, Santiago and Camaguey in Cuba, Veladero, Cap. Haitien and Juana Méndez in Haiti, Martinique, Baltimore, San Francisco, Curacao, Chicago, Jacksonville, Frankfurt, Toronto, Ottawa, Aruba, La Guayra, Veracruz, Turks and Caicos Islands, Port of Spain, Los Cayos (Haiti), Kingston, Mexico City, Maracaibo, and Cadiz.

It also has Honorary Consuls in Australia, Africa, the French West Indies, the Dutch West Indies, Argentina, India, Lebanon, Belgium, Colombia, Costa Rica, Cuba, China, Chile, Newfoundland, Denmark, Canada, Ecuador, Egypt, El Salvador, Brazil, Mexico, Israel, the United States, Spain, France, the United Kingdom, Greece, Scotland, Haiti, Holland, Italy, Jamaica, Norway, Panama, Paraguay, Perú, Portugal, Puerto Rico, Switzerland, Sweden, and Uruguay.

V

DEPARTMENT OF EDUCATION AND FINE ARTS

This department is responsible for educational services and, in general, everything that pertains to scientific, literary and artistic activities in the nation. The supreme authority in the field of public education is the National Council of Education, of which the Minister of Education is Chairman, ex-officio. The other members of the Council of Education are appointed by the President and serve for a period of four years.

Public education is divided into the following branches: Primary, High School, Normal, Vocational and University. Primary education is compulsory for children over seven and under fourteen years of age.

The progress achieved by the Republic during the Era of Trujillo in the field of public education, as demonstrated by the following data, is truly amazing:

In 1930 the budget for the Department of Public Education and Fine Arts amounted to $1,062,231.90. In 1951 it was DR$4,229,397.60. In 1930, the total number of schools in the country was 526. By 1950 the number had increased to 2,695. In 1930, school enrollment totalled 50,739. In 1950, the total enrollment is 256,149.

At the beginning of the Trujillo Era there were 68 grade schools. Today there are 207. In 1930, there were only 6 high schools and normal schools. As of this year there are 45. In 1930, university enrollment totalled only 379 students. At present there are 1,916. Ninety percent of the teachers in grade schools are Masters of Arts or Bachelors of Arts.

In 1930 there were 218 graduate Bachelors of Arts. In 1950 the figure was 1,020. In 1930 there were 116 vocational courses. In 1950 there were 658.

In 1950 the number of grade-school pupils was 209,885, which is an enrollment of 83% of the children of school age.

In 1930, 1,887 certificates and diplomas were awarded. In 1950 the number of certificates awarded by the National Council of Education was 6,645.

During the Trujillo Era several large, healthful and beautiful buildings have been constructed for normal, graduate and vocational schools. Some have sports fields, auditoriums, lecture halls and similar improvements.

During the Trujillo Era the following educational and cultural institutions have been established: the School for Advanced Studies in Accounting; the National School for Physical Education; the National Conservatory of Music and Public Speaking; the Primary Music School; the National Symphony Orchestra; the National Arts Theatre-School; the Musical Lyceum Pablo Claudio; the Gallery of Fine Arts, and the Osvaldo Bazil Institute of Poetry in San Cristóbal, along with several night normal schools for workers.

The Department of Education and Fine Arts has a well-organized Social Welfare service that attends to the needs of impoverished students. It was established by Generalissimo Trujillo as part of his enlightened policy of aid to youth.

Free breakfasts are provided to students under Law No. 2193 of 1944, the Regulations promulgated by the Executive Power governing the functions of the National Committee on Breakfasts for Students, and Decree No. 6245 of 1950. Clothing is provided to needy students in accordance with the provisions of Decree No. 6616 of 1950.

Free breakfasts are provided in all primary schools, high schools and many elementary and emergency Schools.

The breakfast and clothing services are entrusted to a central agency called the National Committee on Students' Breakfasts and Clothing. Its activities are supervised in communities and sections of townships by the Boards and Sub-Boards on Students' Breakfasts as well as by the Societies of Parents and Friends of Education. In 1950 over 15,000 students benefitted from this important Social Welfare service.

Since 1950, the Department of Education and Fine Arts has been engaged in an interesting Cultural Extension Program, whose final objective is the encouragement of cultural and artistic activities designed to further the spiritual progress of the masses, especially through public centers. This program includes concerts, exhibits of books by Dominican authors, lectures on our most important authors, exhibits by Dominican painters, and comedies and dramas presented by the National Arts Theatre-School.

The Department of Education and Fine Arts is determined to carry to the farthest corners of the Republic these manifestations of art and culture so that not a single person will remain in ignorance of the aesthetic appreciation which ennobles the human mind.

A National Committee for Physical Education, consisting of a chairman, a secretary and five members, is devoted to furthering the physical education of students through out the entire Republic. As in the case of the Committee on Students' Breakfasts and Clothing, Boards, Sub-Boards, and Societies of Parents and Friends of Education cooperate with this Committee.

The following achievements, numbered among the most important recent contributions of President Trujillo toward the education of the Dominican people that is so near to his heart, reflect his progressive policies in the field of education.

The reorganization of the courses and curricula of primary, intermediate and high schools; the establishment of two Rural Normal Schools in San Cristóbal and Santiago for the purpose of training teachers who are to work in rural areas; the initiation of seminars for inspectors, principals and teachers; the establishment of five public libraries for the purpose of promoting culture in the capital city; the splendid plan that envisages the construction of fifty buildings for primary and normal schools and was initiated in 1950 with the construction of the magnificent School Palace in La Romana; the creation of the Housing Board for teachers and officials of the Department, designed to facilitate the purchase of homes on the installment plan, which so far has already benefitted 18 teachers during the few months of its existence; periodic salary increases for teachers and officials of the Department, on the basis of length of service; the award of the Order of Duarte and the Order of Trujillo to 75 teachers for outstanding accomplishments, and the creation of the Trujillo Award for teachers who have distinguished themselves in the difficult and selfless task of combatting illiteracy.

The remarkable progress achieved in the field of public education has been paralleled by an astonishing progress accomplished by private or semi-governmental schools and institutions. Among the latter, the following schools in Ciudad Trujillo are included: Colegio Santo Tomás, Colegio La Salle, Colegio Luis Muñoz Rivera, Colegio Serafín de Asís, Colegio Santa Teresita, Colegio Santo Domingo, Colegio Quisqueya, the Salesian School ,the Institute of Commerce, the Gregg Institute and the Luis C. del Castillo Business School. In Santiago there is the Colegio del Sagrado Corazón; in San Cristóbal, the Colegio San Rafael; in La Vega, the Colegio de la Inmaculada Concepción. All of these schools are directed by members of various religious orders and provide splendid education in accordance with the governmental programs.

THE UNIVERSITY OF SANTO DOMINGO

The University of Santo Domingo is the oldest in America.

The island of Hispaniola, which was discovered by Christopher Columbus in 1492, was not only the site of the first political and administrative capital in the New World but also of its first cultural institutions.

In 1502 the Franciscan Fathers undertook teaching activities in the island's capital. They started with primary education for children and later broadened their curriculum to include higher studies in Philosophy and Theology.

In 1510 the Franciscans were followed by Dominican fathers, and by 1518 the latter had established the Dominican Convent for the training of novices and other students.

However, since earliest times education was not the exclusive province of the religious orders. In a Royal Decree dated February 24, 1513, which is perhaps the oldest document relative to public education in America, it is ordered that "the children of Indian chiefs of Hispaniola who show good aptitude shall be taught the art of Grammar and other subjects by Hernan Xuares, Clergyman."

In 1530, Bishop Ramírez de Fuenleal obtained authorization from the Empress for the establishment of a public school "where the children of the natives may learn reading, writing and Grammar." Perhaps Bishop Fuenleal intended to establish a center with the category of one for General Studies since in the request addressed to the Empres he mentions the teaching of "arts and theology" in addition to Grammar.

However, the Dominicans were the first to obtain for their center of studies the classification of a University. At their request, Pope Paul III in his Bull, **"In Apostolatus Culmine"**, dated October 28, 1538, raised the center of studies maintained by the Dominican Fathers in their convent in Santo Domingo to the category of a University, officially established thirteen years before those in Mexico and Lima, which were the first such institutions established on the mainland of the continent.

The Papal Bull of Paul III granted to the University of Santo Domingo the same privileges enjoyed by that of Alcalá in Spain. It was authorized to award all kinds of degrees in its different schools to religious as well as lay students. It was given the name of Royal and Pontifical University of Saint Thomas Aquinas.

About 1801, at the peak of its activities, the University had to close its doors when the capital was occupied by the French troops under Toussaint Louverture by virtue of the Treaty of Basle which ceded the island of Hispaniola to France in 1795.

In 1815, six years after Spanish rule had been restored by an uprising of the Dominican people, the University was reopened. But it was now an institution for lay students and was influenced by the liberal ideas emanating from the Cortes or Spanish parliament at Cadiz. During this period, while the illustrious Núñez de Cáceres was its first Rector, many students from Puerto Rico, Cuba and Venezuela flocked to our University.

But a few years later, while Bernardo Correa Cidrón was Rector, the Haitian invasion again closed the University. In his visit to the University, Boyer, the Haitian leader, undoubtedly viewed the continuation of such a center of traditional Hispanic culture with suspicion. On the surface, he expressed "great interest in the preservation of this center of learning", but no sooner had he left the city than he began to implement his inflexible orders: general conscription for all youths, especially those of university age. In 1823, with the exodus of students from its lecture halls, the University was closed.

Still, the activities of the ancient institution did not die out completely. As has occurred elsewhere under similar circumstances, efforts were made to continue some of the courses outside of the closed doors of the University. For example, several distinguished men, headed by Archbishop Valera y Jiménez and Dr. Moscoso, conducted classes in their own homes.

When the Haitians were driven out of the country in 1844 and the Dominican Republic was founded, the subsequent state of war and the poverty of the national treasury impeded the full restoration of the University. But some higher studies were maintained on a restricted basis. Interest in the preservation of the ancient and glorious institution was unequivocally expressed during the Haitian occupation by Representative Federico Peralta, who proposed to the Constituent Assembly in Port-au-Prince its restoration. His effort proved futile.

In 1845, barely a year after the establishment of the Republic, the government created a Latin School in the University. Two years later, a School of Philosophy and a School of Mathematics were added.

After the second restoration of the Republic in 1865 an effort was made to reorganize the curriculum. President Cabral ordered the establishment of a Professional Institute which, after a rather sporadic existence during its early years, was considerably reinvigorated in 1882 when it was reorganized by the President of the Republic, Dr. Fernando Arturo de Meriño. Following the generous and noble suggestion of Hostos, Meriño himself became the First Rector of the renovated institution.

Thenceforth, the Professional Institute had the organization, schools and curriculum proper to a University. It awarded the same academic degrees as the University itself, except that of Doctor.

The staff of the Professional Institute included the most distinguished names in the nation's cultural life such as Meriño, Galván, Arvelo, Hostos, Tejera, and Nouel. Some of these men later continued to teach at the new University.

Finally, in 1914, by official decree of Provisional President Báez, the Professional Institute became the University of Santo Domingo. Although from the academic viewpoint it was to be a continuation of the center established in 1866, this official action constituted recognition of the preeminent place of honor that our University deserves because of its historic tradition.

DEPARTMENT OF PUBLIC HEALTH AND SOCIAL WELFARE

This Department is responsible for the supervision and direction of the Public Health and Social Welfare services. The Republic is divided into 21 Public Health Districts, each under a Doctor of Medicine, a specialist in Public Health, who is a graduate of the University. There are several health inspectors in each District who enforce sanitary regulations under the supervision of the Medical Officer of the District. All government hospitals, dispensaries and maternity clinics, except those of the armed forces, are supervised by this Department. It also supervises private clinics and the blueprints for all proposed public or private buildings are submitted to it for review and authorization.

Prior to 1930 there were only 10 hospitals and clinics in the Republic, with a total of 484 beds. In 1951 there are 51 hospitals with a total of 5,919 beds.

In 1930 there were 12 medical dispensaries. In 1951 there are 123.

In 1930 the budget for the Department of Public Health amounted to only $317,733.00. In 1951 it amounts to DR$5,$321,535.41.

In 1930 there were only four maternity hospitals in the Republic with a total of 30 beds. At present, the Maternity Hospital of Ciudad Trujillo alone has a total of 375 beds and every important city has maternity wards providing efficient service gratis.

During the Trujillo Era the following medical and public health institutions were established: two hospitals and several dispensaries for tubercular patients; two Children's Hospitals; the Institute of Oncology; a Cardiology Ward in the Juan Pablo Pina Hospital in San Cristóbal; a Central Blood Bank; eight local emergency clinics; a Visiting Nurse Service for post-natal assistance; and several laboratories.

The Department of Public Health conducts permanent preventive and curative campaigns against yaws, malaria, venereal diseases, tetanus and enteric infections. It is able rapidly to combat any epidemic outbreak, as was recently demonstrated in the campaign against equine encephalomalacia which was completely wiped out in less than five months.

The sale of narcotics is only authorized for persons having a certificate from the Department, and their prescription is subject to very strict regulation.

Social Security

Prior to 1930 there was no officially organized and supervised Public Welfare Service in the Dominican Republic.

With the exception of the meritorious work performed by Father Billini on his own initiative, every achievement in this field is owed to President Trujillo.

His work in the fields of Public Welfare and Social Security is so vast that any comparison with the achievements of prior administrations is impossible. Vastness cannot be compared with nothingness. Among the exclusive achievements of the Trujillo Era in these fields there are included the following: pre-natal, natal, and post-natal care for women; compulsory health and work accident insurance; the defraying of burial expenses for the needy; child welfare services, etc.

Prior to the Trujillo Era the Government had never built housing developments for workers nor undertaken to raise their standard of living. Up to the present, 329 houses have been built in the principle cities. Each is a modern, beautiful and healthful dwelling with sufficient ground for a garden. The construction of 500 more in different cities during 1951 is planned.

These dwellings are constructed with Government funds and sold to workers or employees in monthly installments of from DR$14 to DR$35 per month, depending on the type of dwelling.

The Dominican Social Security Fund is a completely new institution which has progressed in an astonishing manner during the few years of its existence, as is demonstrated by the following data.

The average number of medical services rendered annually is 1,000,000. In 1950, 1,019,424 medical and dental services were provided to 455,148 persons. The Fund maintains its own facilities in order to provide these services, such as polyclinics, infirmaries and mobile units, in addition to maintaining endowments in private hospitals. It maintains 248 beds in its hospitals and polyclinics, 205 beds under contract in Government hospitals as well as 152 beds in private clinics. At present it has a total of 605 beds, and this figure will soon be increased when the modern hospital that it is constructing in Ciudad Trujillo is completed.

Health insurance covers doctor's visits, treatments, medicine, financial assistance and burial expenses. About 25,000 persons receive dental care (extractions, fillings and prophylaxis). In order to provide these services, the Fund maintains its own offices and mobile units in addition to endowments in accredited dental offices. The maternity services include pre-natal visits, natal care and aid to nursing mothers. The services of the Fund for work accidents cover doctors' visits, treatments and hospitalization. 10,823 persons are covered by health insurance.

The low-cost kitchens established by Trujillo serve more than 1,000,000 meals per year, and 7,000,000 bottles of milk and over 1,800,000 rolls of bread are distributed gratis among the poor.

The Department of Social Security is also responsible for Children's Nurseries and Reformatories.

Toward the end of 1950, President Trujillo submitted a bill to the National Congress proposing the inclusion, within a single Government department, of the Departments of Health and Welfare and the Department of Social Security. The bill was passed and the Department of Public Health and Social Security was established as of January 1, 1951.

DEPARTMENT OF PUBLIC WORKS AND IRRIGATION

Public works, including the construction of highways, bridges, public buildings, aqueducts and irrigation projects are under the Department of Public Works and Irrigation. The following data give a good idea of the vast scope of President Trujillo's achievements in this field since 1930.

Prior to 1930, 857 kilometers of highways had been built, including 292 kilometers of the Duarte Highway, 260 of the Sánchez Highway, 175 of the Mella Highway, and 130 kilometers of other highways, including the 61 kilometers of the Luperón Highway. The total cost of these highways amounted to DR$12,133,966.50 and the average cost per kilometer was DR$14,158.65.

That year saw the initiation, by virtue of a decree of President Trujillo, of the construction of the great highway network which the country now possesses, covering 3,277 kilometers.

Before the Trujillo Era there were only 84 permanent double-lane bridges, subdivided into 11 steel bridges totalling 2,514 feet of structure, and 73 reinforced concrete bridges totalling 5,378 feet of structure.

In 1933, in the Trujillo Era, the construction of permanent bridges was initiated and up to the present date 272 permanent double-lane bridges have been constructed, subdivided into 18 steel bridges totalling 7,262 feet of structure, and 254 reinforced concrete bridges totalling 18,859 feet of structure.

In 1930 the Republic did not have a single port where large ships could dock. In 1950 there are splendid ports at Ciudad Trujillo, Puerto Plata, San Pedro de Macors and Barahona. At present, a large port is under construction in Haina and a naval base is being built for our warships.

Prior to the Trujillo Era, the existing irrigation projects were carried out by the sugar companies and other private firms. Governmental activity in this field was limited and amounted to three canals which irrigated only 48,000 tareas (1).

From 1930 on, truly important irrigation projects were carried out in the Republic methodically and scientifically, and some that the prior administration had been unable to finish have been completed. As of this date, the total area under artificial irrigation with government canals amounts to 1,837,883 tareas. The following table is presented for purposes of comparison:

(1) One tarea equals 600 square meters.

PRIOR TO THE TRUJILLO ERA

Canals Constructed	Area Covered
3	48,000 tareas

TRUJILLO ERA

Canals Constructed	Area Covered
41	837,883 tareas
Canals Under Construction	**Area Covered**
7	647,000 tareas
Canals Planned	**Area Covered**
11	305,000 tareas
Total of Canals Constructed, Under Construction, and Planned	**Area Covered**
59	1,789,883 tareas
Grand Total	**Area Covered**
62	1,837,883 tareas

The Irrigation Service covers twelve Districts. The Dajabón Irrigation District, comprising an area of 35,300 tareas, is served by the Juan Calvo, Río Limpio, and Guayajayuco canals. The Villa Isabel Irrigation District, comprising an area of 95,000 tareas, is served by the Villa Isabel and La Antona canals.

The Valverde Irrigation District, comprising 60,000 tareas, is served by the Mao-Gurabo Canal. The privately-owned Bogaert Canal, whose 3,000 litres per second capacity serves an area of 30,000 tareas, is located in the latter District.

The Santiago Irrigation District includes the following important canals: the Presidente Trujillo Canal, which irrigates 8,000 tareas; the Navarrete Canal, serving an area of 200,000 tareas; and the Amina Canal, whose 16,000 meters of length serve an area of 22,000 tareas.

The La Vega-Duarte District comprises the Jima Canal, serving 70,000 tareas; the Masipedro Canal, which will serve 32,000 tareas; and the Yuna Canal, which irrigates 270,000 tareas.

The San Cristóbal Irrigation District includes the Nizao-Najayo Canals serving an area of 45,000 tareas, and the Haina Canal, now under construction, which will irrigate 100,000 tareas.

The Baní Irrigation District comprises the Marcos A. Cabral Canal, which serves an area of 100,000 tareas and the Ramfis Canal, which covers 16,000 tareas.

The Azua Irrigation District comprises the Hernán Cortés, Estebanía-Las Charcas, Ibarón, Tábara, Los Toros, Yayas, Bastidas, Villarpando, Monte Grande, Padre Las Casas and Los Corozos Canals, serving a total area of 69,833 tareas.

The San Juan Irrigation District includes the San Juan, Mijo and Guanito Canals, which irrigate a total of 69,453 tareas.

The Las Matas de Farfán Irrigation District comprises the following Canals which serve a total area of 94,950 tareas: El Pinar, El Cercado, Olivero, Matayaya, Barrero, Tocino-Sabana Cruz, and Rancho Pedro.

Public Buildings

In this brief account of the public buildings constructed during the present Era we shall limit ourselves exclusively to those that deserve special mention because of their size and importance. Thus, in the capital, we find the Presidential Palace, a splendid architectural triumph of incomparable beauty, the largest building in the entire island, which houses the offices of the President and his Cabinet; the Justice Building, a three-story reinforced concrete edifice whose interior is decorated with large allegorical murals, and contains all the judicial offices of the city; the Communications Building, a four-story building of reinforced concrete; the Model Market, Slaughter House, Refrigeration Plant and several lesser markets; parks; the headquarters of the Fire Department; the luxurious unsurpassable Hotel Jaragua; the annex to the Headquarters of the National Office of Statistics; the Cement Plant with its installations, which has a productive capacity of 1,200 barrels of high-quality cement per day; the Municipal Incinerator; the National Institute of Agriculture; the University City, Trujillo's greatest achievement in this line, where magnificent buildings house the different schools of our Alma Mater which is the most ancient university in the New World; the buildings of the Departments of Education, Public Health and Social Security, Labor, and the Bureau of Internal Revenue; Doctor Martos

Hospital, the recently constructed Maternity Hospital, Doctor William A. Morgan Hospital, Santo Socorro Hospital for Tubercular Infants, Doctor Salvador Gautier Hospital, Ramfis Hospital, the Headquarters of the National Police, the Nuncio's Palace, the Normal School for Boys; the Normal School for Girls; the Zoo; Ramfis, Julia Molina and José Trujillo Valdez parks; the large-scale improvements and annexes to the buildings of the Senate, the Department of Foreign Affairs, the Administrative Council, and the Chamber of Deputies, to mention but a few.

In keeping with the desire or our illustrious President that the vast plan for reconstruction should encompass all our national territory, all of our nation's cities and municipalities have been provided with modern public buildings to meet all their needs. For example, the following were constructed in the city of Santiago: the Department of Justice Building, Ulises Espaillat Normal School, Estrella Ureña Hospital, the Governor's Mansion, a dispensary for tubercular patients, and buildings for the municipal government. Among the important public buildings constructed in San Cristóbal we find that of the Department of Justice, a new church, the Institute of Agriculture, the Hotel San Cristóbal, the Normal School, two magnificent hospitals, the Governor's Mansion, and the headquarters of the National Police.

All the cities of the Republic are provided with whatever hospitals, school buildings, and municipal buildings they need.

It should be pointed out that the public buildings we have mentioned do not represent the total number of such buildings constructed by the Government, but only a part of those constructed under the supervision of the Department of Public Works and Irrigation, inasmuch as many others were built under the supervision of other Government Departments.

Plan for Dominicanization of Frontier Areas

This plan, whose patriotic inspiration will be praised not only by this generation but even more by future generations, if that is possible, includes the construction of cities embodying all modern comforts and luxuries. Humble hamlets have given way to the fine buildings of modern cities. Among the buildings in Elías Piña, we find that of the Provincial Government, the Municipal Building, that of the Department of Justice, the Postal and Telegraph Building, the Public Works Building, the headquarters of the National Police, Schools, the Electric Plant, the Hotel, the Amusement Park, the Jail, and the parish church.

Among the buildings in Jimaní there are school buildings, a Customs, Immigration and Protocol Building, the Postal and Telegraph Building, the headquarters of the National Police, the Municipal Building, the parish church, the hotel, and fifty private brick dwellings.

Dajabón has the following buildings: a two-story school building, that of the Department of Justice, the Provincial Government Building, and an Electric Plant.

Neyba has buildings for the Provincial Government, Government Offices, and a Jail.

Aqueducts were constructed in the following cities and municipalities during the Trujillo Era: San Francisco de Macorís, La Vega, Cotuí, Santo Cerro, Moca, Montecristi, Villa Isabel, Dajabón, Monseñor Nouel, Valverde, Puerto Plata, Altamira, Salcedo, Villa Trinitaria, Villa Bisonó, Esperanza, Santiago Rodríguez, Loma de Cabrera, El Puerto (Jarabacoa), Villa Altagracia, Yamasá, San Cristóbal, Baní, Azua, San Juan de la Maguana, Las Matas de Farfán, Elías Piña, El Llano, Barahona, Cabral, Duvergé, San José de Ocoa, Jimaní, Neyba, San Pedro de Macorís, Hato Mayor, El Seibo, Higuey, Miches, Sabana de la Mar, Bayaguana, and Monte Plata.

Military Posts

In accordance with the plan to provide water and electric power to several military posts, projects have been successfully completed at: Guaroa, Los Amaceyes, Cruz de Cabrera, Vara de Vaca, Cabeza de Agua, Paso Massacre, El Limón, Paso de los Cacaos, La Palmita, Sombrero, Dajabón, La Vigía, Pedernales, Bánica, Jimaní, Tamarindo, Don Miguel, Los Arroyos, Pedro Santana, Las Lajas, Los Algodones, Villa Anacaona, Restauración, La Peñita, Montecristi, Agua Negra, Paso Viejo de Libón, El Corozo, Alto de la Paloma, Don Juan, La Colonia, El Corte, Tierra Nueva, Guayabal, Malpaso, Capotillo, Loma de Cabrera, Banano y El Copey.

Projects designed to provide water and electric power are almost completed at the following military posts: Los Pinos del Eden, Puerto Escondido, Cacique Enriquillo, Granada, José J. Puello, Tierra Virgen, Aguacate, and Villa Aida.

Small Water Supply System

The construction of small water supply systems has been continued vigorously. The majority of these water supply systems are operated by means of windmills. They consist of a well, a windmill, a concrete tank with a capacity of 3,500 gallons, and a concrete trough. Water supply systems of this type have been constructed in the following places: Hatillo Palma, El Limón, Canca la Piedra, Maizal, Guazumal Abajo, Loma de Guayacanes, El Aguacate, Las Lavas, Gurabo de Mao, Gurabo de Monción, El Guamal, Canao Abajo, Jaiquí Picao, Loma Quemada, Judea, Pedregal, Río Verde, Pajonal, Bonagua, San Francisco, San Francisco Arriba, Los Quemados, Gurabo Adentro, Zamba de Sabaneta, Licey al Medio, Pontezuela, Los Higenitos, Celestina, Cuesta Arriba, Pajonal No. 1, Sabana Mulas, Los Yareyes, Gurabo de Peña, Jacagua, Cacique, Las Caobas, Hundidera, Licey Don Pedro, Boca del Maizal, El Rubio, Cañada Bonita, Los Higueritos, Peladero, Los Copeyes, and Gurabo de Jacagua.

Water supply systems are nearing completion at the following places: Guanábano, Vicente Noble, Canoa, Arroyo Dulce, Los Toros, Bate Verde, Hoya del Caimito, El Mamey, Estero Hondo, Sabana del Corozo, Sabana Grande, Hatillo San Lorenzo, Laguna Grande, Sierra del Guano, and Juan Sánchez.

DEPARTMENT OF ECONOMY AND COMMERCE

This Department was created by Trujillo. It is responsible for all matters pertaining to commerce, banking, industry, mineral resources and other aspects of the national economy. The following agencies are under the Department of Economy and Commerce: the Office of the Superintendent of Insurance, the Bureau of Statistics, the Commission for Coffee and Cacao, and the Register of Trademarks.

There are 21 Chambers of Commerce, one for each province.

The Government maintains 20 textile industries schools, one toy manufacturing school, and one barbers' and manicurists' school.

The mineral survey section of the Department has recently discovered in Cotuí excellent quality iron, gold, silver and gold-bearing pyrites. Gold has also been found in Miches, and coal deposits have been discovered in Imbert, Altamira and El Cercado.

The Bureau of Statistics has all the modern equipment necessary in order to render efficient service. It administered the census for 1950 with complete success. All data relative to our country may be readily found in the Bureau of Statistics.

COMPARISON OF IMPORTS AND EXPORTS
(1930 and 1949)

Value of exports in 1930	$15,530,979.00
Value of exports in 1949	$73,748,548.00
Value of imports in 1930	$ 9,790,033.00
Value of imports in 1949	$46,013,551.00

BANK ASSETS IN 1950

Banco de Reservas (Reserve Bank)	$40,631,096.94
Banco Central	$30,435,132.77
Banco de Crédito Agrícola e Industrial	$ 7,761,757.13

The following figures are eloquent proof of the success of the monetary policy of the Trujillo Administration.

MONEY IN CIRCULATION

December 1936	$ 4,000,000.00
December 1948	$41,094,000.00
December 1949	$49,193,000.00
December 1950	$58,241,000.00

DEPARTMENT OF THE TREASURY AND PUBLIC CREDIT

The Department of the Treasury and Public Credit has been the instrument used by President Trujillo in order to strengthen the public treasury. The disorder in the nation's finances had originated there; Trujillo made it the starting point for his campaign to bring order to them. He brought about a veritable revolution in the fiscal field. He put an end to fraud and corruption. He imposed morality and rectitude. He substituted technical and scientific methods for the prior empirical ones. He simplified and reformed.

This Department is the general accounting office of the nation. The following agencies are under its jurisdiction: the Office of the Comptroller General; the Treasury; the Internal Revenue Bureau; the General Customs Office; the Office of Identification and Registration; the Office of Public Credit; the Office of Inheritance and Endowment Taxes; the Office of the Superintendent of Banks, and the Monetary Board.

In 1950 the total personnel of this Department numbered 1,677.

The arduous and colossal achievements of President Trujillo in the field of our national finances have been fully described in the chapter relative to our Financial Independence.

DEPARTMENT OF AGRICULTURE, LIVESTOCK AND SETTLEMENT

The great progress achieved by the nation in its recent agricultural development is demonstrated by the following figures: in 1950, 48% of the nation's territorial surface was under cultivation — that is 37,737,975 tareas were used for agriculture and for livestock.

The plan for mechanization of agriculture which was initiated in 1949 has yielded truly amazing results. Over 250,000 tareas have been prepared for planting by means of tractors, plows and harrows provided by the Government.

The plan for settlement of agricultural areas has been carried out very successfully, as may be appreciated from the following data. In 1935 the total population of our agrarian colonies amounted to 3,611 persons, of whom 909 were settlers. At present, the population of those colonies is 54,791 persons, including 12,949 settlers. In these colonies there are over 10,000 houses and 57,215 head of cattle; the figure for the poultry population is 146,930.

After satisfying their own requirements, these colonies sold over DR$7,000,000 of produce.

The agrarian clubs have a membership of 24,100 and have 60,000 tareas under cultivation.

The Department of Agriculture, Livestock and Settlement has its own Veterinary Laboratory where various biological products for combatting diseases of livestock are prepared. Subsequently, these products are sold at cost to breeders.

In 1935 President Trujillo initiated the program for distribution of government lands among impoverished farmers. Up to the present, 3,232,177 tareas have been distributed among 97,105 farmers.

The comparative figures for agricultural production during the late 30's and 1949 are as follows: Sugar, 1936, 432,391,298 kilograms—1949, 475,674,146 kilograms— cacao, 1937, 21,256,917 kilograms—1949, 26,000,000 kilograms; rice, 1937, 39,093,275 kilograms —1949, 51,094,941 kilograms; peanut oil, 1937, 57,527 litres—1949, 2,631,854 litres; bananas, 1939, 6,126,298 bunches—1949, 16,732,003.

Through the recent establishment of the Catarey and Rio Haina plantations, which are owned by Dominicans. future sugar production will be greatly increased.

The livestock industry is important. There is sufficient beef and dairy cattle to meet the needs of the country, with a sizeable surplus for exportation.

DEPARTMENT OF LABOR

President Trujillo's interest in the welfare, progress and improved standard of living of the workers led him to establish a Department of Labor as an independent agency within the Cabinet and to promulgate laws designed to protect workers by establishing minimum wages, Sunday rest, maximum work hours, accident insurance, unemployment and prior notice compensation, and other benefits derived from the Rights of Workers.

The trade unions in the different cities of the Republic have formed local federations. The degree of harmony between management and labor is such that despite the fact that the workers' right to strike is recognized by Law there have been no strikes. Disputes between management and labor are amicably settled through the good offices of the Department of Labor. Prior to 1930 there was no legislation to protect workers.

THE JUDICIAL POWER

One of the most important and renowned achievements of the Trujillo Era is the manner in which the law courts operate completely free from any political influence whatsoever. Trujillo has given the country an efficient, prompt and economical judicial system.

The following comparative data are indicative of the progress achieved by our judicial system.

In 1930 the budget for the Department of Justice amounted to only DR$525,019.84. In 1951 it amounts to DR$1,923,092.00.

In 1930 there was a Supreme Court and 3 Apellate Courts. In 1950 there was a Supreme Court and 6 Apellate Courts.

In 1930 there were only 13 Courts of First Instance. In 1950 there ware 26.

In 1930 the Superior Land Court consisted of 3 magistrates, 4 judges of original jurisdiction, sitting at Ciudad Trujillo, 1 government attorney with power to act as prosecutor, 1 Recorder of Deeds, and 1 Director of Cadastral Surveys with a staff of surveyors to review and control all surveying operations.

In 1951 the Land Court consists of a Superior Court with 5 judges, 8 judges of original jurisdiction sitting at Ciudad Trujillo, and 7 judges of original jurisdiction of whom 1 sits in San Juan de la Maguana, 1 in San Cristóbal, 1 en San Pedro de Macorís, 1 in La Vega, 1 in San Francisco de Macorís and 2 in Santiago.

It has 5 Recorders of Deeds: 1 in Ciudad Trujillo, 1 in San Cristóbal, 1 in San Pedro de Macorís, 1 in La Vega and 1 in Santiago.

There is a government attorney, who has 2 assistants and a staff.

The Land Court also has an Office of Cadastral Surveys, with a Director and his staff, who are responsible for the review and examination of cadastral surveys made in the Republic. It is empowered to approve or reject such surveys.

Cadastral Surveys

The total area of the Republic that has been surveyed amounts to approximately 20,000 square miles (82,370,752 tareas), that is, 52.95% of the national territory.

Court Decisions

During 1950 the courts handed down 92,014 decisions, subdivided as follows:

Civil Suits	4,639
Commercial Cases	296
Criminal Cases	1,329
Minor Infractions	55,534
Misdemeanors	30,216

Our penal system is subdivided into the technical functions relative to the operation of prisons which are within the province of the Office of the Attorney General of the Republic, and the administrative functions which are the responsibility of the Quartermaster General of the National Army.

The duties of the Attorney General of the Republic, in addition to those stipulated in the Law on Government Departments, consists principally of the supervision and direction of the officials of the Department of Justice and sheriffs or marshalls. It is therefore empowered to issue instructions, serve writs, enforce regulations and prosecute any of the aforesaid officials whenever such action may be warranted.

ADMINISTRATIVE COUNCIL OF THE DISTRICT OF SANTO DOMINGO

In 1950 the budget of the Administrative Council of the District of Santo Domingo amounted to DR$2,131,425.39.

In 1930, with the exception of El Conde Street, all the streets of the capital were in poor condition. In 1951 nearly all the streets of Ciudad Trujillo are either paved with macadam or asphalt, or are in the process of being constructed.

In 1930 the Public Market in Ciudad Trujillo was a national disgrace. At present there are three model markets of which the one located on Avenida Mella is the equal of the best in the world.

In 1930 the municipal slaughterhouse was a disease focus and health hazard. In 1951 Ciudad Trujillo has a model Industrial Slaughterhouse. It is efficient and sanitary and has a great capacity. It is equipped with ample modern cold-storage facilities and all the necessary machinery and equipment.

Prior to 1930 the colection of trash and garbage was in the hands of private firms and the municipal government. Horse-drawn vehicles would collect the trash and garbage which was dumped in the sea at a distance of three kilometers from Independencia Park.

In 1951 garbage is collected by specially built trucks and taken to a modern incinerator located in the outskirts of the city.

THE COLUMBUS MEMORIAL LIGHTHOUSE

A book on Trujillo and his administration would be incomplete if it failed to mention his persistent efforts in behalf of the construction of the symbolic Columbus Memorial Lighthouse which will embody America's desire to render fitting tribute to its illustrious Discoverer. But the Columbus Memorial Lighthouse will be more than that. As President Trujillo stated in the speech he delivered when the great project was initiated, "besides a deserved tribute of reparation out of justice by America," it is to be a solemn and "moving demonstration of universal solidarity." In addition to serving as a monument to perpetuate the glory of the Great Admiral and an archive for preserving the precious heritage of the documents relating and describing his great feat, together with his immortal remains, it will constitute a permanent appeal for friendship and unity among the nations of this hemisphere.

J. L. Gleave, the English architect who is its designer, has explained the following regarding the Columbus Memorial Lighthouse.

The geographical location of the Columbus Memorial Lighthouse marks it as the future great crossroads of world air and sea traffic.

The memorial will have a Chapel where the remains of the Great Discoverer will be entombed in Dominican soil, fulfilling his own wish regarding the land of his burial.

The monument of marble and bronze now in the Cathedral in Ciudad Trujillo will be transferred to the Memorial Lighthouse. The Memorial Lighthouse will contain libraries and museums enshrining valuable historical relics of Columbus' times.

The general structure will be low in comparison with the surrounding terrain, in order that the monument may be protected against earthquakes and hurricanes. The fragility of modern structures is inadmissible in a building whose very nature demands that it be a lasting structure.

The plan of the memorial, making splendid use of lights, has been developed with precision, simplicity and strength worthy of the great monuments of our times. The concept is symbolic, but is happily wedded to the project's simple architectural beauty.

The form of the building expresses in architectural abstraction the motivating idea. Like the pyramids and other great monuments down through the centuries, the

Memorial's architectural character is not limited to one particular period but is designed for all time. Seen against a dark sky, its silhouette reminds the viewer of the Egyptian sphinx, an Aztec serpent or an elemental nature sketch. By day, clothed in marble, under smiling skies, its symbolical modern design will constitute a clear and simple architectural note supported by its darkened canyons.

Looking backward through the canyons above the cross and by the Ozama river, the visitor will see Ciudad Trujillo, the first city of the New World, whose capitol is in a direct line with the axis of the Beacon. On either side of the canyons in the Monument, he will see chapels, libraries and museums, safe perennial repositories for relics of the Columbian era.

The principal Chapel will be located in the very heart of the monument, and will house in its center the mausoleum containing the remains of Christopher Columbus. Every evening, at twilight, and in all kinds of weather, an organ will play a requiem to Columbus which will be repeated seven times, starting with a barely audible rendition flowing from the Chapel and the canyons and ascending in crescendo simultaneously with the beams cast by the great cross as they rise in the night.

The Chapel as well as the canyons will remain still and shrouded in darkness, and the only illumination will come from the star of Columbus which will shine in the ceiling at a height of 70 feet, casting a dazzling light over his tomb which is at present in the Cathedral and will be transferred to the Memorial.

From the roof of the lighthouse the visitor will be able to see the historic Ozama river and the city, framed by the mountains on the distant horizon.

The first glimpse of the lighthouse from the air will tempt the imagination —a gigantic cross inlaid in the ground—an idea expressed in heroic proportions—the sign of the cross which came to the New World— the first air cross.

As his airplane descends, the visitor will see the huge bulk of the Monument emerging from the Great Cross, and as he notes the double symbolism he will grasp the magnitude of the lighthouse against the background of its setting and the diminutive figures beneath.

Standing on the Great Cross, he can see, over the open space and the rostrum, toward the end of the lighthouse, the huge walls on which are engraved the words of Columbus:

"You shall set up crosses on all roads and pathways, for as God be praised, this land belongs to Christians, the remembrance of it must be preserved to all time."

The enormous bulk of the monument, embodying Modern Progress, extends from east to west, symbolizing the route sailed by Columbus as he brought Christian civilization, to the point where the arms of the cross open, as if pointing to North and South America.

The Columbus canyons emerge from the center of the monument, as if guiding and controlling the advance of Progress from his times, in the form of a cross.

Those canyons, which are large crevasses, are the entrances to the lighthouse. Only 12 feet wide and with 30-

foot high rough red walls, they will transport the visitor to the dark times of Columbus' imprisonment and the prevalent superstitions of his times.

Crowning Modern Progress, and directly over the tomb in the chapel, there is the Altar of Progress, with its 21 symbolical rays and revolving light, reflecting the symbol of the lighthouse across the mouth of the port.

From the far ends of the lighthouse, the open space and the flags of the 21 American Republics on the Great Cross may be viewed.

At night, the parallel themes of Columbus and Modern Progress will be expressed by means of lights whose reflections will be projected from the main part of the lighthouse which rests on the immense paved Great Cross. The latter, in turn, will be located in the center of the International Park covering some 2,500 acres which have been set aside permanently by the Dominican Government for that purpose.

Toward the west, a wide road leads to one of the locks of the Ozama river, opposite historic Ciudad Trujillo.

Twenty-one avenues, each representing an American republic bearing the name thereof, originate at the Great Cross. The International Park and all the area to the east of the Ozama river, which was the first site of a city founded by Columbus and is the location of the first Catholic church built in the New World, will be planned with a view to preserving a proportionate and esthetically harmonious relationship with the old city and enhancing the view of the Great Cross from the air.

Contributions

In addition to donating the site for the Columbus Memorial Lighthouse project, the Dominican Republic has contributed the following sums for the design and initiation of its construction and for publicity relative thereto:

1926	$300,000.00
1931	40,000.00
1933	15,000.00
1938	2,098.13
1939	15,000.00
1948	350,000.00
1948	300,000.00
1949	200,000.00
Total	$1,222,098.13

Other American Republics have contributed as follows:

Mexico, January 1945	$20,000.00
Honduras, August 1945	5,358.00
Nicaragua, November 1945	3,623.13
Panama, November 1945	3,035.34
Costa Rica, August 1946	3,360.49
El Salvador, August 1946	9,040.60
Brazil, October 1948 (1,495,381 cruzeiros)	79,881.46
Ecuador, December 1948	8,787.55
Total	$133,086.57

Dimensions of the Monument

The Columbus Memorial Lighthouse is designed in the form of a giant prone cross, the axes of which are divided by two canyons. The dimensions of the monument are:

a) Total length	778 feet
Length of the arms of the cross	167 feet
Maximum total height	131 feet
Width of canyons	13 feet

b) The Great Chapel, octagonal in shape, will have a width of 53 feet and a height of 73 feet;
c) The Great Cross, which has already been completed and will surround the monument, has a length of 2,264 feet; in length the arms of the cross measure 545 feet.
d) The International Park has an area of 932 acres.

Symbolism

a) The Central Canyon of the Memorial which is to crown the monument over the tomb of Columbus, will consist of a single powerful light and will have 21 vertical rays of concrete symbolizing the 21 American Republics;
b) 21 avenues will begin at the head of the cross, one for each American Republic, and the length of each will be 656 feet, depending on the conformation of the land;
c) Besides the Great Chapel of the Admiral, the monument will have 21 lesser chapels or halls, each repre-

senting an American Republic. They will be located behind the main Chapel and will be reached from the longitudinal canyon. They will accomodate libraries, a Columbia museum, exhibits of native art, archives, etc.

d) The lights cast from the canyons will form a luminous cross in the clouds. On clear nights the beams will rise to a height of 3,000 feet;

e) The flags of the 21 American Republics will be displayed permanently around the monument's principal stairway. The stairway, which has already been completed, consists of 21 steps;

f) The monument will have its own electrical equipment, modern telecommunications facilities, and a great electric organ which will play a requiem to Columbus each evening, starting in a low key and gradually rising simultaneously with the beams cast from the canyons until the "Gloria in excelsis!"

UNIVERSITY CITY

On November 15, 1943, in a message to the Senate, President Trujillo requested the appropriation of DR$500,-000 from the budgetary surplus of that year in order to start construction of the University City. On November 26, the Congress approved the President's proposal and on February 7, 1944, ground was broken in the Independencia District, near the sea and to the west of Ciudad Trujillo. There the University City will occupy an area of 360,000 square meters. The blueprints and supervision of the project have been entrusted to architects and engineers of the staff of the School of Exact Sciences.

On August 17, 1947 the buildings that had been constructed as of that date were inaugurated in a ceremony held in one of the amphitheatres of the Doctor Defilló School of Medicine. The ceremony was part of the program celebrating the inauguration of General Trujillo, the first Doctor **Honoris Causa** of the University of Santo Domingo, as President of the Republic for the term of office from 1947 to 1952. The University City is the permanent home of the University of Santo Domingo, the oldest institution of higher learning and professional studies in America.

On the campus of the University City, covered with beautiful trees and extensive gardens, six buildings have already been completed, namely, the School of Medicine, the School of Pharmacy and Chemistry, the School of Dental Surgery, the Institute of Anatomy, the Laboratories of the School of Medicine, and the Central Seismological Station. Still to be constructed are the buildings of the Schools of Law, Exact Sciences and Philosophy, the Library, the building to lodge the different Institutes attached to the diverse schools, the Sports Stadium, which will accomodate 10,000 spectators, and the building for garages and warehouses.

Up to the present, thanks to President Trujillo's efforts, the government has invested DR$1,857,141.98 in this project.

The buildings already constructed are large, chaste in their style, well lighted and ventilated, and house the different schools of the University of Santo Domingo together with their auxiliary sub-divisions, and the administrative office.

At present, all the University's schools together with their auxiliary sub-dxivisions are located in the University City. Their enrollment is as follows: School of Philosophy (present academic year 1950-51), 163, of whom 12 are foreigners; the School of Law, 478; School of Medicine, 768, of whom 24 are foreigners; School of Pharmacy and Chemistry, 277; School of Dental Surgery, 139; and the School of Exact Sciences, 502.

The total enrollment during the present academic year at the University is 2,333, the largest in its long history. During the present academic year, a total of 95 foreign students are enrolled in the different schools; the largest single group consists of Puerto Rican veterans of the World War II studying under the G. I. Bill of Rights of the United States.

The following Institutes and auxiliary sub-divisions are attached to the various Schools: School of Philosophy—the Institute of Anthropological Research, the National Museum, the Institute of Journalism, and the Music and Folklore Section; School of Law— Institute of Comparative American Legislations; School of Medicine— the Institute of Anatomy, the Bacteriology, Parasitology, Physics and Chemistry, and Histology and Pathological Anatomy Laboratories; School of Pharmacy and Chemistry —the Pharmacy and Chemical Research Laboratories and the Institute of Botany; School of Dental Surgery — the Dental Clinic and the Dental Laboratories; School of Exact Sciences —the Institute of Geographical and Geological Research, the Central Seismological Station; and work shops.

The Library, which is appropriately lodged in the University City, contains over 500,000 items including books, reviews, newspapers, maps, miscellaneous publications, etc. The Cultural Extension Program of the University is carried out through the Library. Up to the present, under the latter program, many exhibitions have been held in different cultural centers of the Capital and other cities.

The University has an Athletics Department which promotes and supervises the intra-mural athletic activities of the students in the various schools. On the campus there are basketball, volley ball and tennis courts, and a Sports Field offers facilities for baseball, softball, football and all field and track events. Every year the teams of the diverse schools compete in organized events and sports relations are maintained with foreign educational institutions.

COMPARATIVE STATISTICAL DATA FOR THE YEARS 1930 AND 1950-51

In 1930-31 the University's enrollment was 379.

The Government appropriation for the year 1930-31 for the University amounted to $50,897.00.

Enrollment for the present academic year 1950-51, is 2,333 students.

The University's budget for 1950-51 amounts to DR$672,746.07, including a government appropriation of DR$460,000.00.

TOURISM

Generally speaking, mistaken or incomplete ideas prevail abroad regarding the progress achieved by the Dominican Republic during the past 20 years which are rightly named the Trujillo Era.

A casual visitor or a person whose knowledge of the Republic is derived exclusively from newspapers or reviews finds the material progress achieved by Trujillo, as evidenced by countless highways, steel and concrete bridges, public buildings, schools, avenues and parks, and the University City, irrefutable tangible proof of our astounding achievements during such a brief period. But that is not all. The real progress achieved by the Republic is visible in the enormous moral progress, intellectual accomplishments and civic development which cannot be gauged in terms of modern buildings or automobiles.

That progress is to be found in education, from the relentless campaign against illiteracy up to and including the formidable impetus given to university studies, in administrative efficiency which has virtually banished fraud and corruption, in the social transformation of the masses rendered possible by raising their standard of living. In brief, that progress is subtle, the product of a solid and permanent peace, not readily visible to the eye but sensed in business prosperity, in the steady expansion of industry, in the contentment of workers and farmers, and in the tranquility which prevails throughout the country.

The Dominican Republic of today is ideal for tourists, especially from the viewpoint of geographic location as well as air and sea transportation facilities.

In addition to its proverbial hospitality, the country offers ideal facilities for rest and amusement, beautiful scenery and monuments of unsurpassed historical value. The modern government-owned hotels, the Jaragua, the San Cristóbal, the Maguana, the Montaña, the Jimaní and that under construction in Boca Chica, one of the most beautiful seaside resorts in the Caribbean, offer the visitor every modern comfort.

The Department of Tourism, which functions as an agency of the Government of the District of Santo Domingo, offers every facility to tourists, including automobile trips to the most picturesque places in the country at reasonable prices set by the Government, with chauffers who speak English, French and Spanish.

Together with the most priceless historical colonial landmarks in America, the tourist can observe the progress achieved in a country enjoying order, peace, and full business prosperity.

THE DOMINICAN PARTY

Visitors to our principal cities will find that in each of them one of the most beautiful, spacious and modern buildings is the local headquarters of the Dominican Party.

They are true centers of culture, and each has an auditorium adequate for the presentation of cultural events.

The motto of the Dominican Party is **Probity, Liberty, Work, Morality.** Its emblem is the Royal Palm.

AGENCIES OF THE PARTY

At present there are: a Central Governing Board, 20 Provincial Boards, a Board for the District of Santo Domingo, 68 Area Boards, 13 Municipal District Boards, 6 Sectional Boards, 155 Urban Subordinate Boards and 1,568 Rural Subordinate Boards.

Enrollment since the Establishment of the Party
As of December 31, 1950

Provinces	Men	Women	Total
Azua	14,656	9,828	24,484
Bahoruco	11,843	5,874	17,717
Barahona	17,691	12,917	30,608
Benefactor	29,368	9,054	38,422
Distrito de Santo Domingo	68,213	46,677	114,890
Duarte	48,065	27,609	75,674
Espaillat	44,832	16,467	61,299
La Altagracia	21,959	11,881	33,840
La Vega	63,411	39,062	102,473
Libertador	10,061	4,859	14,920
Montecristi	27,155	11,499	38,654

Provinces	Men	Women	Total
Puerto Plata	44,344	23,124	67,468
Samaná	22,644	14,131	36,775
San Pedro de Macorís	27,605	14,032	41,637
San Rafael	10,141	6,611	16,752
Santiago	85,125	43,427	128,552
El Seibo	30,302	21,691	51,993
Trujillo	53,915	27,230	81,145
Trujillo Valdez	23,184	15,799	38,983
Independencia	5,234	4,363	9,597
Total	659,748	366,135	1.025,883

During 1950, 39,397 persons enrolled in the Party, of whom 22,507 were men and 16,890 women.

The following Provinces had the largest enrollment:

Provinces	Men	Women	Total
Distrito de Santo Domingo	2,294	3,033	5,327
Puerto Plata	1,187	2,728	3,915
Trujillo	2,204	1,366	3,570

PART FIVE

COMMENTS

CHAPTER XX

OPINIONS OF PROMINENT PUBLIC FIGURES AND WRITERS ON A FULL-LENGTH PORTRAIT OF TRUJILLO

THE PRESIDENT OF THE REPUBLIC

Ciudad Trujillo,
District of Santo Domingo
April 22, 1939

The Honorable Abelardo René Nanita
Senator of the Republic
Ciudad Trujillo.

Dear Friend:

Thank you for your book "A Full-Length Portrait of Trujillo." It is a dispassionate appraisal of my life as manifested by my deeds, whose appreciation is in the hands of the sincere critics who are able to evaluate and arrive at conclusions that are just to one who has performed those deeds in fulfillment of a duty and pursuing an ideal.

I value and appreciate your work as the product of a conscientious writer and a sincere friend. It is yet another stimulus for performing my duty wherever circumstances place me, firm and resolute in upholding my faith and in defense of the cause.

Most sincerely yours,

Rafael L. Trujillo

THE VICE-PRESIDENT OF THE REPUBLIC

Ciudad Trujillo,
District of Santo Domingo
April 21, 1939

Mr. Abelardo R. Nanita
Ciudad Trujillo.

My esteemed friend:

I was very happy to receive the copy of your book "A Full-Lentgh Portrait of Trujillo" (second edition) that you were kind enough to send me.

As a fervent admirer of the strong personality of the great Dominican whose outstanding characteristics are unprecedented and stand unparalleled in our history, I again read with pleasure and interest the book which you wrote some time ago in order to present to the world the noble figure of Rafael Leonidas Trujillo Molina. As a result of reading this second edition, I am able to fully appreciate your statement in the preface, that, despite the more than seven years which have elapsed, "I have not had to modify a single opinion expressed", because all that you said before regarding the past was just and true and what your mind foresaw on the basis of the then prevalent reality has been amply fulfilled.

My dear friend, please accept my congratulations for your deserved success, together with my thanks for the copy of your excellent book which you so graciously sent to me.

Very sincerely,

(signed) Manuel de Jesús Troncoso de la Concha

OSVALDO BASIL

Río de Janeiro, May 11, 1939

The Honorable Abelardo R. Nanita
Senator of the Republic
Ciudad Trujillo, Dominican Republic

Dear Abelardo:

Even though I haven't heard from you for some time, upon learning that you have earned the praise of your colleagues in Congress because of the success achieved by your masterly "sketch" of Generalissimo Trujillo, I feel compelled to write to you. You have indeed molded a moral and physical sculpture of the Chief Executive. Your work "A Full-Length Portrait of Trujillo" presents the harmonious whole, body and soul. It is the biography of the Generalissimo. You have cast a bronze medallion of Trujillo for posterity. It deserves to be engraved on a plaque on the front of the Baluarte del Conde, the cradle of our Liberty and the sanctuary of our national honor. No other biography of Trujillo captures details and focuses the character of the whole man as yours does, and in such a few, straightforward words. Your pen gains inspiration from the incentive of your patriotic admiration of Trujillo. It is a pity that you do not write more often. You should undertake to write the history of our country from 1924 to 1939, when Trujillo spontaneously stepped down from the Presidency. Above all, you should encompass in those fifteen years of our nation's life Trujillo's achievements and the history of his eight years at the nation's helm. In order to do justice to the steely, intrepid and dazzling personality of Generalissimo Trujillo it would be necessary to convert the writer's pen into a sculptor's chisel, and to be a master at synthesizing. I believe that you, using the style of sketch, could write that chapter in the history of our nation's political life. You should write such a book. It would be the finest heritage for your children.

Most cordially,

Osvaldo Bazil

J. B. LAMARCHE

Ciudad Trujillo,
District of Santo Domingo
May 9, 1939

Mr. Abelardo R. Nanita
Ciudad Trujillo

My esteemed friend and colleague:

Your splendid work, "A Full-Length Portrait of Trujillo", has afforded me great pleasure. I have been able to appreciate in your clear and succint style the brilliance of your intellect which has undertaken, most appropriately, the difficult task of sketching the outstanding representative of our political and social milieu, Generalissimo Rafael L. Trujillo Molina.

This book, in which its literary style and its characteristic psychological basis vie for the reader's attention, is beyond all praise.

You have succeeded in bringing to tangible dimensions the noble figure of the great man, the first citizen, the eminent statesman, the peerless patriot, the hero of peace and work, in undying prose of amazing accuracy and colorful realism.

Therefore, in this brief letter, I offer you my heartiest and most sincere congratulations.

Affectionately yours,

J. B. Lamarche

TRUJILLO

(Review by Daniel Henríquez Velázquez)

"To Daniel Henríquez Velázquez, whose fervent loyalty to Trujillo, identical to mine, has forever cemented the bonds of our old friendship".

A. R. Nanita

Abelardo René Nanita, a writer of extraordinary talent, wide culture and elegant style, whose artistic accomplishments raise him to the level of our country's finest authors, has recently published the fourth revised and enlarged edition of his excellent biography of Rafael Leonidas Trujillo Molina.

Perhaps unintentionally, in this biography of the noblest Dominican statesman, Nanita has included by way of dedication a brief, moving and accurate biography of his subject's distinguished mother. Thus, in corresponding chronological order a concise record of the life of that virtuous mother is joined to the analytical biography of the son.

In my opinion, regardless of whether the author planned it that way, it constitutes a novel and happy twist. Nanita, in accordance with the routine followed in works of this kind, includes at the beginning of his book some brief **Biographical Data** on Generalissimo Trujillo which were published several years ago by Rafael Vidal, another fervent admirer of Trujillo and a famous Dominican author.

The biographical data, thanks to the magic rhetoric of the author and notwithstanding their brevity, constitute a comprehensive sketch of the character, life and achievements of Trujillo. But even when describing the long line of distinguished forebears of the great statesman, they fail to define exactly the immediate reason for Trujillo's greatness —the outstanding virtues of his mother.

This Nanita supplies with his masterly touch, arousing in the reader the first and one of the keenest and most enduring emotions of the entire book.

Nanita dedicates his book to Doña Julia Molina de Trujillo in the following words: "To the sweet and self-effacing goodness of his mother, calm possessor of all virtues." Those words, that are worthy of Homer, sum up the virtuous life of his mother and are the best possible explanatory preamble to the heroic and impressive greatness of her remarkable son, whose character truly dazzles owing to the variety of its aspects and the quality of its merits.

Thus favorably disposed, the reader admiringly contemplates the glorious panorama of the life of the great statesman, unfolded in the personal, brilliant style of the author which portrays his mastery of the profound and simultaneously pleasant and attractive subject.

Nanita is unstinting in expressing his fervent devotion to his subject. Undoubtedly, in the final analysis, every biography is the product of a deep and sometimes hidden admiration which moves the author to write it. A biography's subject may command public sympathy or odium, but even when the author harbors the latter feeling his antipathy is so intertwined with some particularly interesting fact that, despite himself, he is moved to admiration.

But it is a common failing of biographers that they allow themselves to be carried away by their own fervor, either intentionally or otherwise, and are overly partial, stressing only the favorable aspects and even indulging in hyperbole to the detriment of the lustre of their subject's real, albeit minor, virtues.

Nanita is not guilty of that lack of objectivity that generally converts biographies into worthless panegyrics instead of what they should be —a faithful portrayal of the subject's life.

Undoubtedly, the fact that the merits and virtues of Trujillo rise above the inaccuracies and falsehoods of any possible hyperbole made it easy for Nanita to avoid that error.

But it is likewise true that the author was scrupulously careful to resist the promptings of his personal fervent devotion to Trujillo. Thus, he has succeeded in giving us an accurate portrait of the man and not a conventional photograph. With this he has made one of the most important contributions to the history of our country since ,as Emerson stated, properly speaking, there is no such thing as history —there is only biography.

Nanita observes: "The outstanding basic characteristics found in him today are the same that were found to an astonishing degree in the young man: leadership, organizing ability, an awareness of responsibility, patriotism, intelligence, valor and, above all, a thirst for glory and a passion for outdoing his own achievements."

Nanita has cast a splendid medallion which portrays pre-eminently the soldier, the statesman, and, in brief, the public figure in its entirety. For our better understanding, Nanita shows us both sides of the medal, and then we encounter the paradoxical side of Trujillo.

It is precisely that paradox which constitutes the essential element of his greatness— the ability to be, depending on circumstances, "implacable yet gentle, a realist yet a dreamer, audacious yet patient, quick yet calm", and at all times capable, just and good.

He has that ability, since he is the tenacious, conscientious and deliberate architect of his life, his work and even of his glorious place in history. Nanita describes that aspect of the man marvellously. He says: "His self-control has made Trujillo the arbiter of his own life, wherein all actions, even those requiring the greatest audacity, are performed with calm deliberation. Frank to the point of bluntness, his words are sometimes as cutting as a diamond, but equally clear."

Thus, deliberately, he has produced that "splendid development, a prodigious fulfillment of the capabilities of one predestined by Divine Providence to accomplish a mission at once singular, of transcendental importance and superhuman in scope: the complete regeneration of a nation, involving both its reconstruction in the material order and its moral rehabilitation. Such a task unquestionably calls for a genius and a hero whom we may call a veritable superman."

No painter, no sculptor could portray his spirit as faithfully and accurately as Nanita has done.

If all of us, the old and true friends and fervent admirers of Trujillo were to attepmt to select the best historical monument to the glory of our illustrious leader, I am certain that we could not find one to equal Nanita's work as the interpreter of our ideal.

In brief, Nanita's book is the product of his patriotism, since, as someone once said, the biographies of great men are mankind's best teachers.

DEAMBROSIS MARTINS PRAISES A. A. NANITA'S BIOGRAPHY OF PRESIDENT TRUJILLO

Accomplished writer reviews the highlights and analyzes, as does the author, those achievements of President Trujillo which he considers most outstanding.

Ciudad Trujillo,
August 1948

Mr. Abelardo R. Nanita
Ciudad Trujillo

My esteemed friend and colleague:

I am very grateful for the copy of your interesting and splendid book **Trujillo**, which I received and have just finished reading.

That will give you a good idea of the interest (literally speaking) that your disconcertingly engrossing book aroused in me. No task is more difficult and arduous than that of writing the biography of a contemporary who is still making chapters in the history of his life and who is forever astounding us by his breath-taking ascent toward the loftiest summits.

In the foreword you wonder —and most properly— which are the greatest contributions of President Trujillo to his country's glory.

I agree with you that they are these three:

1) The Trujillo-Hull Treaty, followed by the liquidation of our foreign debt.

2) The delimitation of the boundary with Haiti, followed by the building of cities on the border.

3)His idea of a League of American Nations which, as I stated in a lecture which I gave recently at the Ateneo Dominicano, came to fruition at the Ninth Conference of American States held in Bogotá which produced the Charter of the Inter-American System, together with its corollary, the "Trujillo Doctrine", which embodies a valuable thesis relative to the recognition of governments and the rupture of diplomatic relations.

I found the biography data on Generalissimo Trujillo prepared by Rafael Vidal very interesting. I was very happy to have accepted the invitation of the Ateneo of San Cristóbal to repeat in that glorious city, the cradle of the Republic's first Constitution and the birthplace of our greatest statesman, my lecture on "The Role of the Dominican Republic at the Bogotá Conference", through an invitation giving me the opportunity of praising in his very birthplace our hero's achievements and his international policy during recent years.

Trujillo's lineage, French, Spanish and Dominican, which you describe so brilliantly, as well as his innate creative vocation, have made him one of the most extraordinary personalities in America. You portray him with a true artist's brush, and future biographers will have to turn to your book because of its honest accuracy. I especially cherish the following lines which are most accurate:

"Well built, soldierly without being pompous, of average height, the President cuts a good figure. His winning ways not only assure receptiveness on the part of his hearers but are such as to influence even his enemies..."

"Another of President Trujillo's remarkable assets is his ability as a conversationalist. Spiced with a mordant sense of humor, his words come in a free and easy manner. Neither pompous nor stuffy, in the company of intimates he does not stand on protocol..."

That is precisely how I saw him on Saturday morning, August 21, when I had the honor of visiting him, and that afternoon at Estancia Ramfis, where I was honored and privileged in also meeting his wife, Doña María de los Angeles Martínez de Trujillo. She also impressed me greatly with her unaffected distinction and the patrician simplicity with which she received her guests. It is indeed refreshing to see simplicity in the great; it is the maximum expression of their human qualities.

I chatted with both of them, and I, who during the thirty years of my career as an international political writer, foreign correspondent and diplomat in Paris have become accustomed to interviewing the great —Kings, Presidents, Queens, and Foreign Ministers— can affirm that President Trujillo is a true gentleman, and his wife is a fine and gracious lady. I am not yet acquainted with her books, but my old friend Vasconcelos—an old colleague of mine whose judgment is unerring and whose accolades are rare indeed— spoke to me about the First Lady's gifts as a writer and thinker in tones of admiration which aroused my curiosity to such a degree that I ventured to importune her with a request for copies of her books.

I could devote numberless pages to comment on the interesting chapters of your book that are so skilfully correlated. I am at a loss as to which of the two parts I prefer—the one devoted to the man, abounding with so many very interesting details which make us love him all the more, or the one referring to the Statesman, which is so well documented and will stand me in good stead for future studies on the Dominican reality. Surely you are aware that the fifth chapter,entitled "An Eternal Frontier", embodies the essence and the perfection of your splendid work, and deserves special comment. This chapter complemented the lecture I had read relative to the same topic given by Mr. R. Emilio Jiménez, Editor of **La Nación**, who is one of the most distinguished Dominican thinkers.

I intend to again examine your book and send you further comments when I return to my routine in Europe, resuming my work in Paris or Geneva.

I observe that your book has been translated, and that there are several English editions of it. It might be worthwhile to also translate it into French for its distribution in Europe where President Trujillo's personality is not suficiently known. I sincerely believe that your book offers a very complete panorama of the distinguished Dominican President and his historical achievements. Perhaps the addition of a final chapter devoted to his colossal achievements through the present year 1948 would complete your book by embodying the real essence of a life completely dedicated to the greatness of his country and the glory of America.

I congratulte you for having so ably and accurately portrayed your illustrious compatriot, whom you have served and continue to serve with loyalty and thoughtfulness worthy of this, my spontaneous and admiring praise.

Very cordially yours,

Dr. Carlos Deambrosis-Martins

A MASTERLY WORK

A Revealing Sketch of a Statesman

We draw the attention of our readers to the biographical sketch which is published below, written by the discerning Dominican figure, Abelardo R. Nanita, for which we are indebted to the courtesy of Enrique Deschamps, our distinguished colleague and friend. Although the latter had already informed us of the exceptional gifts, culture and talent of Mr. Nanita, as well as of many other representative citizens of the progressive Caribbean republic (because, willy-nilly, through Deschamps one gets to know all his worthwhile compatriots) we must confess that the sober literary work that we are hereby introducing reveals a writer of clear and solid academic standing, endowed with the unmistakable psychological vein so essential to every author of real stature and the absence of which would be fatal to any man who engages in politics.

We are not familiar with the problems of Dominican politics, but we firmly believe that, no matter what they may be, Mr. Nanita's sketch covers the most important ones.

This sketch tacitly lays down a clear, accurate, definitive and conclusive norm, not for the future but for the present which is so fraught with uncertainty and threatened or assailed by the misery prevalent throughout the world.

It behooves Dominicans to accept as their North Star the line set forth by the extraordinary skill of Abelardo R. Nanita's subtle pen. It is a path that leads to order, the backbone of all governmental administration. That blessing alone, in our times, possesses the incalculable value of being the desideratum of all the nations of the world. It is well known that so many countries are deprived of it that those which do possess it as the Dominican Republic does should make every sacrifice for its preservation.

A balanced budget and a country at peace are the two gifts which Rafael L. Trujillo Molina has brought to his country through his constant and exhausting labors. Any Dominican who wishes to appreciate exactly those two achievements of Mr. Trujillo's is urged to read any more or less reputable foreign newspaper. His eyes will be opened to the tragic truth that in our dark days no other country enjoys such a double blessing. Neither of the greatest nor of the smallest nation in the world can we say what Mr. Nanita expreses so clearly: "The Republic has balanced its budget and peace reigns throughout the country."

Humanity's great sorrows in the present phase of history are no laughing matter. If Dominicans would defend their welfare and their very lives, let them not demur for an instant and let them follow the very wise advice of Mr. Nanita as one. Because undoubtedly in that country there should be but a single common interest—the preservation of that well-being to which President Trujillo has unstintingly given of his skill, physical and moral energy and labors.

Prior to meeting Mr. Nanita, we had heard another authority express himself identically with regard to Mr. Trujillo and the order and progress prevalent in the Dominican Republic. We refer to Mr. Deschamps who, although he did not reveal the broad panorama set forth by Mr. Nanita, made us feel something more than a mere liking for the Dominican leader, awakening in us a sincere admiration for the young President of that noble Caribbean country that has undertaken the task of leadership for universal homage to the Discoverer of the New World. He acquainted us with the intrinsic nature of the mission of that man who assumed office following a disastrous administration and who a few days after had to cope with the most terrible hurrricane in the history of the West Indies which devastated the capital of the Dominican Republic, leaving over twenty-five thousand victims in its wake and over fifty million dollars of material damage.

(From the review "Colón", Nº 18, February 1933, Barcelona, Spain).

A GREAT LITTLE BOOK BY ABELARDO R. NANITA

By Gerardo Gallegos

I must confess with the honesty of a professional writer dedicated to the task of writing for the public that although I was aware of the existence of an extensive bibliography relative to President Rafael Leonidas Trujillo, I have scarcely had occasion to glance at a biography of the Dominican Republic's President. In other words, I have not read any work interpreting his public career and his personal life through an intimate psychological study of the man.

In Cuba, on various occasions, I reveived defamatory pamphlets written by his political enemies. As they were merely insolent and impudent diatribes, I never had the patience to read them through.

However, an occasional detail of his life contained in those pamphlets, despite the perverse intention of the author to distort the truth, far from arousing in me the desired reaction of aversion toward President Trujillo, had precisely the opposite effect, permitting me to catch an intuitive glimpse of a sterling personality. It is likewise true that my spontaneous rejection of the venomous diatribe was due to my first-hand, albeit brief, acquaintance with the Dominican Republic when I visited that country fifteen years ago. At that time I was able to see the clear outlines of today's concrete reality.

The result of all this was to awaken in me a subconscious desire to know fully the personality of President

Trujillo, in all its diverse aspects. At the same time I began to hope that perhaps some day I would have the opportunity of writing a biographical essay on him, setting forth his luminous portrait against the dark background of the hostility against him. I thought that my feeling for the subject, inspired by achievements which could only be wrought by a Titan's will-power, would allow me to write an original biography that would constitute a valuable addition to the Latin American biographies.

But recently, only a few days ago, I discovered that my belief that I could write such an original and successful biography was erroneous.

It would not be possible because after having read a small book, almost an 80-page pamphlet, entitled "A Full-Length Portrait of Trujillo", I find that its author, Abelardo R. Nanita, has written a masterpiece, which cannot easily be improved upon as a psychological study of the illustrious Dominican President. At least I am convinced that, no matter how great my efforts may be, I could never achieve the qualities that render Nanita's "A Full-Length Portrait of Trujillo" a great concise biographic work.

From its very first page it is evident that the book was written by one who, aside from his talents as a writer and I might say as a poet, has closely and constantly observed the glorious career of his subject from the earliest manifestations of his intellectual brilliance to its full fruition. Nanita traces the unswerving path of his subject's will that, like a sculptor's chisel, has been transforming the physical and moral physiognomy of a nation over two decades.

The success of Nanita's book is readily understandable because a biography is a product of intuition, the intuition derived from admiration and love. His book is an artistic creation. But creation is impossible without the aid of a warm and vibrant emotion, such as is found abundantly throughout the 80 pages of "A Full-Length Portrait of Trujillo".

Generally speaking, the biographer dwells on various facts which he considers characteristic of his subject. But were he to allow himself to be carried away by his enthusiasm, his book might well turn out to be not a biography, but an exceedingly long series of anecdotes that could destroy the unity of the subject rather than presenting it as a bust of solid marble. Instead Nanita—a master of modern literary technique whose style is characterized by direct and precise phrases— does without anecdotes, and with bold and accurate strokes paints the full-length portrait of Trujillo with full spiritual depth.

This book contains only eighty pages; they are short like those of a breviary, and like parchments so laboriously drawn by the Benedictine monks of the Middle Ages. It would be difficult indeed to add anything to his work which would set forth a new facet of President Trujillo for posterity. This is a great little book which portrays the essence of his sterling character, and the strong will of the Dominican statesman. In brief, it interprets his ardent ideals of faith and hope in the future of the Dominican Nation.

"A Full-Length Portrait of Trujillo" a biography written ten years ago, was then, is now and ever will be timely.

It is a lasting work because it embodies immutable values in the midst of the changes and inevitable vicissitudes of man's existence on earth. ("La Nación", March 6, 1950).

OTHER OPINIONS

I have derived great spiritual benefit from reading "A Full-Length Portrait of Trujillo", a product of the gifted pen of Abelardo R. Nanita, the distinguished writer. It is the best work ever written on the multi-faceted personality of the Generalissimo.

Luis E. Aybar R.

(La Opinión, 1938)

A. R. Nanita's "A Full-Length Portrait of Trujillo" has been included in the bibliography for teachers in the new curricula for Primary Education prepared by the Department of Education and Fine Arts, and in the high school curricula, in the fifth term social studies as well as in the bibliography for teachers for the third term National History and Geography courses.

Abelardo R. Nanita is not a journalist reporting on a statesman, nor a novelist transforming reality through the spur of fantasy, neither is he an historian judging a man in the light of historical perspective, and he certainly is not an essayist generalizing and building doctrinal concepts or cultural strata with data.

He is a loyal friend of a head of a nation admiration and devotion to whom have made him his biographer.

F. Ulises Domínguez

("Listin Diario", August, 1938)

"During the time when I was Ramfis' tutor I read several biographies of Trujillo. The one which most impressed me for its excellent quality was that by Abelardo R. Nanita, an old friend of the President, whose pen was able to capture, hold and describe most happily the complex personality of one of the greatest men of Latin America." (José Almoina, in his book **I Was Trujillo's Secretary**, Buenos Aires, Argentina).

APPENDICES

APPENDIX I

It seems fitting at this point to quote certain salient passages of the letter addressed to Professor Luic C. del Castillo on November 25, 1916 by the author, expressing his oppostion to the demands of the United States and the erroneous interpretation by that Government of Clause III of the Convention of 1907.

Santo Domingo
November 25, 1916

Prof. Luis C. del Castillo
Santo Domingo.

Distinguished Friend:

I enclose a translation that I made for **La Nación** of the original English text of the Treaty between the United States and Haiti. In my opinion an examination of that text leads to the following conclusions:

a) The interpretation of Clause II of the Dominican-United States Convention relative to "public debt" which you defend so brilliantly, is correct. The United States Department of State is of the same opinion, as is readily evident from a careful examination of Article 8 of the Treaty with Haiti.

b) The United States Department of State bases itself on our non-fulfillment of the aforementioned Clause in order to present its demands, desiring to give elasticity to the provisions of the Convention. If our Ministry of Foreign Affairs concurs it would be tantamount to an acceptance of the opportunistic interpretation by the United States as a legal one. If its opinion were accepted, the scope of that international instrument would be unlimited and its provisions would be the springboard for new and more formidable demands. For example, the same argument used to demand the establishment of a Financial Counselor and a Police Corps controled by the President of the United States, in order to compel us to observe Clause III, could later be used in order to demand control of public education, postal services, telegraphic communications, the courts and so on **ad infinitum**, because what national activity would not be subject to United States control since all of them constitute, to a greater or lesser degree economic factors? If international treaties were subject to such opportunistic interpretation it would not be worthwile to embody so many clauses in them —one alone would suffice.

c) A Comparison of the United States note of November 19 with the Treaty with Haiti shows clearly the disadvantageous position in which the former places us. If it were necessary to partially yield to the demands by the United States and to legalize certain **faits accomplis**, this should be done by means of a new treaty wherein positive benefits could be stipulated, in return for what we would yield decorously. Furthermore, that is the only legal way to solve the conflict. It is true that in its Treaty Haiti yields much in return for very little; but if we were to accept the aforementioned United States note we should be yielding everything for nothing and, furthermore, we would be at the mercy of the United States for an indefinite period.

In conclusion ,in our opinion, the Dominican Government should flatly reject the United States note, because the Constitution does not authorize it to accept the opportunistic interpretation of Clause III of the Convention which is the base of the above mentioned note.

Very truly yours,

A. R. Nanita

(From the weekly "La Nación", I, No. 8, 1916).

APPENDIX II

REPLY OF THE PRESIDENT OF THE DOMINICAN REPUBLIC TO THE COMMUNICATION OF THE DEPARTMENT OF THE INTERIOR OF HAITI DATED SEPTEMBER 9, 1941.

Radiogram

Ciudad Trujillo,
September 10, 1941

His Excellency Elie Lescot
President of Haiti
Port-au-Prince, Haiti.

I have just read with great interest the communication of the Department of the Interior of Haiti relative to the recent frontier incidents, and I have experienced deep satisfaction because of the sincere and truthful manner in which it reparts those incidents. I did not doubt for a single moment that the Government over which Your Excellency presides so efficiently and honorably would regard those events in accordance with what actuallly transpired and with a spirit of sincere understanding. I am convinced that the attitude of your Excellency's Government in this instance will constitute a solid and fruitful basis for the maintenance of friendly relations between our two countries, thus inaugurating a new era of imperturbable cordiality and fruitful cooperation in all fields of activity. With like gratification I inform Your Excellency that the publication of the communication of the Department of the Interior of Haiti has produced sincere satisfaction among the Dominican people, counteracting the harmful effects of distortions of facts which similar incidents occasioned in the past.

M. de J. Troncoso de la Concha,
President of the Dominican Republic

APPENDIX III

QUOTATIONS FROM LETTERS ADDRESSED TO PRESIDENT TRUJILLO BY ELIE LESCOT

On March 16, 1937 he wrote: "My great and good friend: Allow we to again express my gratitude for the thoughtful and courteous kindnesses which your brotherly sentiments have inspired. Out of the goodness of your heart you have divined my anxiety in a difficult financial situation on the eve of such an unexpected departure. How and in what measure can I ever reciprocate the numberless kindnesses which you have bestowed upon me since my arrival on this Dominican soil which you have made so dear to me? I pray that God may grant me the opportunity to some day express my gratitude to you and your dear ones. My family and I are deeply indebted to your generosity and unsurpassed kindness."

On August 22, 1937 he wrote: "I am very near to you but circumstances impede my hastening to you, embracing you and renewing the pledge of my friendship and gratitude in person."

"Five months have elapsed since I left Ciudad Trujillo and, for reasons which you will understand, I did not wish to maintain correspondence with you nor with anyone in the Dominican Republic other than my wife and my son. I am kept under strict surveillance, but you must know that my brotherly sentiments toward you have not changed, nor can they ever change, come what may."

"I have been in Haiti since the 12th of this month. All kinds of measures have been taken here in order to impede my going to Ciudad Trujillo, because of the fear which our friendship inspires in the government."

"On the 13th of next month my family will leave the Dominican Republic, going to the United States by way of Port-au-Prince. Henri, my son, your young protegé, will travel with them, etc."

On February 7, he wrote: "My great and good friend, my brother: I have emerged from the painful Calvary which the bad faith of one of my compatriots tried to inflict upon me. I owe this to the ever greater generosity of your noble heart, because you have wished to put an end to a simple matter which, from the very beginning, could have readily been settled directly in accordance with your wishes."

"I do not know how to express to you my gratitude for your boundless generosity toward me, as evidenced by this most recent proof. Thank you, my brother."

On April 11, 1939, he wrote: "The moment has arrived for me to avail myself of your ceaseless offers in the sense of facilitating my assuming the Presidency of the Republic."

"I have instructed Gerard (1) to request an interview with you, in order that he may personally submit my plans to you, and obtain, on the strength of your brotherly feelings, the financial support and all manner of assistance which may be essential to win. I am absolutely convinced that I can count on you just as you can absolutely count on me. Fidelity and Loyalty even unto death — that is your motto, and it is also mine."

"Such is the attitude that your unquestionable patriotism and perspicacity as a great statesman have inspired you to take, in behalf of the safety of your country and its progress."

On April 11, 1940, he wrote: "I promised you that I would go to Port-au-Prince, but you know full well that I shall take no measures without first receiving a communication or advice from you, which I requested some time ago, either through Pastoriza or through my son, who informs me that he has transmitted to Santanita all my communications."

"One fact must be borne in mind and that is that I cannot remain indifferent to such a situation, because such in-

---

1. Gerard Lescot's eldest son, was at that time Secretary of the Haitian Legation in Ciudad Trujillo.

difference can only help my enemies. On the other hand, to make a trip there in order to initiate a Presidential campaign, I need your indispensable support. Therefore, I rely on you alone, my dear and good friend."

"One fact is indisputable and that is that Vincent only takes decisions when impelled by fear or selfish motives. It is essential to increase, without further loss of time, the fear inspired in him by the presence of Calixte in the Dominican Republic. Without any recourse to arms, it would be desirable to have Calixte, together with many horsemen, seen from time to time in the vicinity of Dajabón and Comendador. A way should be found to have that news reach the Haitian authorities so that they, in turn, may inform Vincent. Calixte should appear to be very busy during these days. Any simulated activity on the part of Calixte will strengthen my hand vis-a-vis Vincent, as I am known to be the only man capable of impeding a movement by Calixte, because of the brotherly friendship which is known to exist between you and me."

"A serious perturbance in the border area at this time could lead to Vincent's resignation, and if I have money available I could easily win over the Representatives and Senators. In the present state of affairs, I think that this is the best strategy to attain the Presidency. My dear and beloved friend, I would appreciate your opinion regarding this plan as soon as possible. You will set my mind at ease."

"At the same time I am working on a plan designed to gradually dislodge the French clergy, who are principally responsible for the differences between our two countries. You are well acquainted with this problem."

"My dear friend, please let me have your opinion as soon as possible by means of a coded cablegram addressed to Pastoriza. I am uneasy over the way things are shaping up and, I repeat, I rely on you alone for indispensable support."

In a letter to his son, Gerard, now in the possession of President Trujillo, Lescot writes: "If you are unable to see my Great Friend, (1) inform him through Santanita that the hour of decision is at hand, and that Vincent is plotting a coup d'etat. He refuses to admit that he should surrender his office. If he comes to realize that it is no longer possible for him to continue in office, he is capable of abetting a military coup d'etat to place Major Armand in the Presidency. My decision not to travel to Haiti annoys him. His plan was to keep me under surveillance in Haiti in order to neutralize me, just as he does with any Haitian whom he regards as a potential successor. The United States is absolutely opposed to Vincent's continued tenure of office. They do not like Armand either. That is why they have deprived Vincent of all means to make propaganda or to take any action. For example: the refusal of the request for the purchase of rifles on deferred credit; the indefinite postponement of the construction of the hotel as well as of the visit by American Catholic clergymen; and the fact that, up to the present, what the decision on the moratorium will be remains unknown. The United States Department

1. Generalissimo Trujillo.

of State is aware of the statement I made to Vincent regarding my succeeding him as President upon the expiration of his term of office, and it approves that statement. Events in Haiti are being closely followed here. However, I am not counting on any direct assistance from the Americans. I rely solely on my Friend. I am biding my time here, until Vincent makes a move to continue in office through a coup d'état. In that event I shall resign in a sensational manner and denounce publicly in the press and over the radio his shameful misdeeds, availing myself of his correspondence with me in which he compromised himself. I shall explain that it is morally impossible for me to continue to serve such a dishonest government. I wish my Friend to know that I have the most absolute and complete faith in his promises, and I repeat that I rely only on him and on God. I should like to know whether my Friend agrees with the plan which I submit in order to proceed as indicated, and if events force me to do so, I shall go immediately, together with my family, to the Dominican Republic in order to organize an armed movement without delay in a SECRET manner."

"In my opinion, it would be desirable that Vincent should feel a certain uneasiness because of the situation in the border areas or due to any other cause. Perhaps that would force him to compromise."

"Abel Leger has been called by Vincent and is going to Haiti with his family. The strategy seems to be that Leger should enter the political fray as one more candidate in order to complicate the situation, thus permitting Vincent to emerge as the decisive victor."

When Trujillo loaned Lescot the sum of $31,250 so that he could replace the exact amount entrusted to him by the Government of Haiti for the purchase of rifles, Lescot wrote to Andrés Pastoriza, the Dominican Minister Plenipotentiary in Washington, as follows: "My dear Pastoriza: I am sending to "El Jefe" (1) through you a copy of the letter which was sent to Port-au-Prince yesterday. It is a very important letter because it refers to the suggestion about which you know."

"In the report attached to the letter I deleted some names lest Port-au-Prince learn who supplied the information therein."

"As I wish to send today, by air mail, the check requested of me by cable and about which you know, I beg you, my dear friend, to do everything possible to aid me because the bank closes at two o'clock in the afternoon. Yesterday I spoke with "El Jefe" and I told him what a great thing he has done for me, saving me from the greatest peril to my future that I have ever encountered."

A MEMORABLE LETTER

Following numerous and repeated public attacks by President Lescot against our country, our people, and our Chief Executive, President Trujillo was compelled to address to him on November 1, 1943 a temperate and well documented letter from which we have copied the following paragraphs:

---

1. "The Chief", meaning Trujillo.

Ciudad Trujillo,
District of Santo Domingo
November 1, 1943

His Excellency
Elie Lescot
President of Haiti
Port-au-Prince.

My dear Mr. President and friend:

At the end of May when I read the speech you delivered on "Flag and University Day", I felt a desire to write to you to express my painful surprise at its veiled attacks and grave threats against me, my Government and the Dominican people.

However, I thought that the appeal to hatred addressed to Haitian students was merely a political expedient and not the true expression of the feelings of the man who was pleased to call me "brother" and who vowed his "eternal friendship" to me.

I asked myself, "How can one reconcile in honest sincerity that frankly hostile attitude with the brotherly affection that my old and dear friend Lescot professed in the past? How can one reconcile those attacks and threats with all the expressions of affection and deep gratitude that he professed in the past unreservedly in all his letters?"

I asked myself, "How can the man in whom such absolute faith had been placed and who was the port of refuge on various occasions demanding the solution of grave and vexing problems today become the target of offensive criticism?"

I confess, my dear President and friend, that I gave you what Americans call "the benefit of the doubt", and that between the recent insult and the sworn friendship I decided in favor of the latter.

However, my faith in my old friend was again shaken when I read another speech —the one which you delivered on September 6, on the occasion of the 41st anniversary of the death of Killick, the Haitian hero.

If your oratory of May 18 constituted a veiled attack against "the noble friend" and the Government which tendered you unfailing and generous refuge, the speech of September 6 was almost a battle cry and a surprising expression of hatred which seems to turn your back on a friendship which I for one have maintained unaltered.

At that time I decided to eventually write to you expressing my sorrow at that radical change of attitude and to point out to you the incompatibility between the recent past which abounded with affection and admiration for me and my Government's policies and the present which is so unjustifiably hostile toward me, my Government, my people.

In the speech of May 18 —a speech which, if you will allow me to repeat, regrettably sowed hatred in the minds and hearts of Haitian youth— you seemed to discard strong bonds of friendship and gratitude and you made me and the Dominican people the targets of words which scarcely hide a deliberate and wounding intention to offend. The implications were so thinly veiled that the Haitian press, in reporting the speech, believed itself to be serving its latent purpose by bitterly criticizing all things Dominican.

My dear President and friend, I need not repeat here those unfortunate words which have become, in Haiti, a rallying point of rancor and a dangerous battle cry, creating there a popular feeling that, fortunately, is far different from that which I have maintained here in behalf of the normal relations existing between our two peoples and in behalf of the cooperative endeavors of our two Governments for democracy.

The regrettable threat that you expressed on May 18 was categorically reaffirmed on September 6 last in the speech which you delivered rendering homage to the heroism of Hammerton Killick. The final part of that speech contains words which would have given Dominican patriots cause for alarm had I not taken precautions to assure that popular reaction not be commensurate with what could have been considered an act of gratuitous provocation.

APPENDIX IV

WHAT IS CUBA'S ROLE IN THE CARIBBEAN WAR?

Undoubtedly, that clandestine and sinister group is even now preparing to strike a heavy seditious blow. Figueres, the former President of Costa Rica, has just returned from Israel, where he purchased large quantities or arms for the Caribbean Legion. For months on end war activities have been at a standstill owing to Arévalo's preoccupation with the elections in his country. Against the will of the people, and availing himself of means running the full gamut from squandering money recklessly to mass coercion of illiterates and the physical persecution of all opposition candidates, he has succeeded in placing Arbenz in power... It is expected that now that the Arévalo régime has consolidated its political power, war will break out among the nations of the Caribbean.

Just as in the United Nations the ever present question is "What incident will set off the Third World War?" the Chancelleries of all these countries are constantly alerted to the next invasion.

War is about to break out again, and the Government of each country is ready. Will they decide to gather their forces and launch a coordinated attack on this or that territory? Or will they prefer to incite internal rebellions? The threads of the plot are tense and vibrant, as in an Ellery Queen mystery. Everyone is suspect, and Havana is one of the centers if not the very vortex of this madness which has seized the men of the Caribbean.

What is Cuba's Role?

Cuba's involvement has grown progressively. Each day she alienates one more nation and her prestige suffers because of her irresponsibility in international relations. President Prío's heritage included Cuba's participation in the Caribbean war "against dictatorships".

Thus, with the knowledge and connivance of all, so that in Cuba and throughout the Caribbean even infants in their cradles knew it, the invasion of Santo Domingo was planned during the administration of Grau San Martín. The preparations were so well advanced that the leaders of the plot against President Trujillo were wont to assure all and sundry in Havana that "the only remaining problem is the maintenance of order once we have overthrown Trujillo."

Such confidence could only be imparted by the highest authority in the land.

When President Prío assumed office, he found that the would be invaders were already installed and armed to the teeth. Juan Bosch, a former eloquent admirer of President Trujillo, a turncoat who had become the leader of the freebooters, hovered near Prío as his **Eminence Grise** and Clausewitz Bosch's anti-Trujillo venom was shared by Dr. René Fiallo, a confidant of the Cuban President. The Presidential Mansion swarmed with members of the Caribbean Legion, and the latter's activities gradually assumed an official hue, which Prío Socarrás had probably never intended.

Prío's inherited entourage was soon increased by the presence of a sinister person endowed with the cunning of a tiger and capable of convincing anyone that he held the key to success. That person was Rómulo Betancourt. In his downfall he dragged along Rómulo Gallegos, who was his dupe. The two went to Havana, and while Gallegos, the writer, made a fool of himself and demonstrated his inability to govern even a children's classroom, Betancourt the politician tightened his tentacles around President Prío.

With characteristic naiveté, the President of Cuba had forgotten that during his visit to Caracas while Betancourt's clique was in power he had been accorded extremely cold treatment, receiving only the barest protocolary honors, merely because he was disliked by the Venezuelan communists. He likewise forgot that during that visit to Caracas a plot to assassinate him while at the Hotel Avila had been uncovered and thwarted... He welcomed the exiles in a fatherly manner, but was incapable of nipping in the bud the transfer to Cuba of Betancourt's rancor and diabolical machinations.

According to reports prevalent in the Caribbean countries, the Government of Cuba is subsidizing the Betancourt and Figueres groups to the tune of $18,000 per month, with the lion's share going to Betancourt since he established his permanent residence in Cuba. (It should be recalled that Betancourt went to Washington and succeeded for some time in embroiling the left-wing clique of the Department of State. But once his plans were discovered by the Americans, he was expelled from Washington. He now resides in Havana ,and as he is the real mastermind and leader of the whole movement, we find that Cuba has the dubious honor of serving as the principal base for the war in the Caribbean.)

Obviously, this is contrary to the wishes of the Government of Cuba, but it has failed to take any decisive measures to disprove the accusations. This explains two ugly versions concerning the death of Chalbaud: that his assasination was masterminded and plotted in Cuba, and that Rómulo Betancourt and Simón Urbina met in Miami recently.

In order to complete the list of countries "democratized" by the Army of Liberation of the Caribbean led by Figueres by virtue of Betancourt's promise that he will make him the Simón Bolívar of Central America, it was first necessary to win the battle of Guatemala. Arévalo is now entrenched in power behind the figurehead of Arbenz. Delgado Chalbaud has been assassinated, in the belief that the Military Junta of Venezuela will fall apart and lose control of that country, and that the moment is ripe for another adventure.

But there are certain obstacles. Let us examine them: 1) The United States will not cooperate in the invasion of any country and is hostile to the creation of a Federation of Socialistic Republics of America; 2) President Trujillo no longer has to cope with the problem of a Haitian government flirting with the Caribbean Legion and threatening the Dominican people with massacres unparalleled in in history; 3) Although there is no connection between the attempt on President Truman's life and the assassination of Delgado Chalbaud, the times are not propitious for assailing Presidential authority in any country; indeed, the opposite is quite true; 4) The Organization of American States is alerted and the Dominican Government has scrupulously complied with all its resolutions and counsels, including those relative to political exiles; 5) The United States Department of State no longer harbors persons of the Lattimore ilk who advise the ruin of "non-democratic" governments by revolution or any other means; 6) the links between Arévalo and international communism have been demonstrated by facts such as Guatemala's voting record in the United Nations; 7) The rumored trip of the President of Cuba to Guatemala on August 12 of this year, if it actually did take place, did not importantly affect the relations between the Government of the United States and that of Guatemala; 8) Although the attitude of the Cuban Government with regard to Puerto Rico was the result of very particular historical reasons, the Cuban gesture has been interpreted as a manifestation of affinity with the anti-United States policy of Arévalo, leading to the conclusion that there exists a plan for consolidating the peoples of the Caribbean, including Puerto Rico, against the United States, with the cooperation of Argentina sought by Arévalo; 9) The moment is not propitious for starting a war, because, following the death of Delgado Chalbaud and the accusations made by the Dominican Republic and Venezuelan diplomats as well as Peruvian government officials, the O. A. S. will most probably initiate a new investigation and will oblige the Governments concerned to cease sheltering groups of exiles and storing arms for the use of one country threatening another, simultaneously imposing recognition of the fact that in the Caribbean area the independence of nations and the sovereignty of Governments constitute an argument formidable enough to render the "export of democracy at bayonet's point" inadmissible.

The Clandestine War

Perhaps war will not break out right now because of the aforementioned reasons. But the activities of spies, diplomats, and the Intelligence Services will multiply. The cold war of contraband, passport forgery, surreptitious movements of exiles and subversive agents will continue in this insane Caribbean. The peaceful citizens of each capital will be unaware of what goes on. The threads of a plotted outbreak of rioting such as that which devastated Bogotá or of an assassination which will shake the nation to its foundations will be woven around them, but all they will read will be the polite statements by the various Chancelleries.

No one sleeps in the Caribbean these nights. Armed to the teeth, the enemies watch each other. Everyone is shadowed. The next step, according to the sinister imaginings of the men of mystery who have intimate knowledge of the Caribbean fever, is the bombing of Caracas by four planes which will take off from Guatemala... It is all a madness, a false rumor, an absurdity, but it is the warp and woof of today's Caribbean tragedy.

And while those machinations take place, the capital question of our times remains unanswered, "What is the Cominform's role in all this?". Neither President Prío nor José Figueres are advocates of Stalinism; but Arévalo and Betancourt... Who knows whence they receive orders to carry out their sinister moves!

The Caribbean is aflame —one more spark in the conflagration set by Soviet Russia. Puerto Rico is in constant turmoil; the other countries are on a war footing, watchfull. Is this not a reasonable facsimile of what Russia is creating in all strategically vital areas? When the whole history of the present Caribbean madness is written, the reader will find, lurking like a poisonous centipede under a stone, the name of a Soviet agent, the supreme mastermind behind the insane frenzy that is driving the Caribbean area toward its own destruction.

(From the "Diario de la Marina", November 19, 1950, Havana, Cuba.)

BIBLIOGRAPHY

Evolución de la Democracia en Santo Domingo, by Rafael L. Trujillo Molina.

Reajuste de la Deuda Externa, by Rafael L. Trujillo Molina.

El Pensamiento de un Estadista, (Discursos, Mensajes y Proclamas), by Rafael L. Trujillo Molina.

Meditaciones Morales, by María Martínez de Trujillo.

Elementos de Derecho Administrativo, by M. de J. Troncoso de la Concha.

Naboth's Vineyard, by Sumner Welles.

Yo fuí Secretario de Trujillo, by José Almoina.

Geografía Descriptiva de la República Dominicana, by J. Marino Incháustegui

San Cristóbal de Antaño, by Emilio Rodríguez Demorizi

Resumen de Historia Patria, by Bernardo Pichardo.

Cuadros Históricos Dominicanos, by César A. Herrera.

Reseña Geográfica, Histórica y Estadística de la República Dominicana, by Vicente Tolentino Rojas.

Visión de un Pueblo, by Gerardo Gallegos.

Un Estadista de América, by Fabio A. Mota M.

Una Pregunta y Cien Respuestas, by A. René Nanita, Jr.